Breaking *Everyday* Addictions

Dr. David Hawkins

HARVEST HOUSE PUBLISHERS

EUGENE, OREGON

BREAKING EVERYDAY ADDICTIONS
Copyright © 2008 by David Hawkins
Published by Harvest House Publishers
Eugene, Oregon 97402
www.harvesthousepublishers.com

Library of Congress Cataloging-in-Publication Data

Hawkins, David, 1951-
Breaking everyday addictions / David Hawkins.
  p. cm.
ISBN-13: 978-0-7369-2341-5
ISBN-10: 0-7369-2341-1
1. Compulsive behavior—Religious aspects—Christianity. 2. Addicts—Religious life. I. Title.
BV4598.7.H39 2008
248.8'629—dc22

2008012040

Printed in the United States of America

08 09 10 11 12 13 14 15 16 / VP-NI / 10 9 8 7 6 5 4 3 2 1

To those who struggle with addictions,
seeking, perhaps time and again,
the courage, resolve, faith, and tenacity
to claim the freedom we are promised in Christ.

Acknowledgments

My experience with addictions began in my childhood, when I heard stories about my paternal grandfather's struggle with the alcohol addiction that ultimately claimed his life. Thank you, Mom and Dad, for sharing those stories with me and for helping me to develop compassion and understanding not only for those who struggle with addictions but also for the innocent victims of addicts. Our conversations were open and frank, and they gave me the freedom to write about such a sensitive topic.

And especially to Christie, my wife: Thank you for again supporting me in my writing. You encourage my creative expression, and you've become a valuable editor. You are a gifted writer in your own right, and everything you say and do makes my writing stronger.

Special thanks go to my friend and colleague, Terry Glaspey, for believing in a book about such a difficult topic. You had the foresight and wisdom to realize that we need to talk about addictions. I appreciate your encouragement more than you can know.

Thanks go again to Jim Lemonds, an extremely talented editor and writer, who has worked with me for years on countless book projects. Jim, your talents always strengthen my writing.

I again thank Gene Skinner, the workhorse who plows through the initial manuscript, reviewing it with a fine-toothed comb. You always make me put in a little more time, but the result is always a better book. Even though I never look forward to your to-do list (especially providing missing information in the notes), you sharpen the book so we are all satisfied with the final product.

Thanks also go to the entire team at Harvest House Publishers, who have labored with me many years now in producing quality books. I know how hard you work for me, and I am indebted to you.

Finally, thank You, Lord, for the ongoing blessing of being able to write. I love writing, I believe You have put urgings and concerns on my heart, and I labor together with You to bless, challenge, and encourage people.

CONTENTS

PART ONE

What Are *Everyday* Addictions?

CHAPTER ONE

A Parade of Everyday Addicts

I did it to myself. It wasn't society...it wasn't a pusher, it wasn't being blind or being black or being poor. It was all my doing.
RAY CHARLES

I'M AN ADDICT. Most of us are.

There, I've said it. Wanting to write about addictions for a long time, I finally received the green light from my publisher.

My publishing team sat around the conference table sipping Cokes, lattes, and bottled water, listening to my sales pitch. Finally, Elisa, one of the editors, asked quizzically, "Can a book about addictions really sell?"

"I'm not sure," I replied, glancing around the room at the concerned faces. "But I do know this: We're a nation of addicts, and it seems like we ought to be talking about it. We pretend that addictions only happen to other people. That's not true."

"There's an image out there," Elisa said, "that if you admit to having problems with an addiction, people will think you're like drug addicts. The kind who steal to support their habit and have lost their teeth, their health, their kids, and their home. They're in such denial about the whole issue that they wouldn't want help if you offered it."

Several team members nodded in agreement.

Kirk, from sales, got up and poured himself another cup of coffee.

"We've drawn this imaginary line," I added. "It's *them,* the addicts, and *us,* the normal ones."

"So," Donna from acquisitions said, "is something wrong with that kind of thinking?" Just then her cell phone rang. "I'm sorry," she said, taking a moment to check the caller before turning her phone off. "I thought I turned this thing off."

"There's a lot wrong with that kind of thinking," I continued. "I want to talk about everyday addictions. The kind that affect each of us. I'm not pointing any fingers, but I like my lattes every day. I like to tell myself coffee's just a passion. But to be honest, I'd have a hard time living without it."

"Sounds familiar," Kirk added, smiling.

"I've also struggled with work addiction, but I like to tell myself I'm just a hard worker. I still carry my Palm with me wherever I go, and my laptop is always within reach."

Donna smiled anxiously. "You're hitting close to home," she said.

"There are the addicts that sit next to us in church or work in the cubicle next to ours. They live next door, and their kids play with our kids. We're afraid to talk about these addictions because we fear being seen as stereotypical drug addicts."

"I'm still not sure I'm getting it," Kirk said impatiently, glancing down at his watch. "Either you're an addict or you're not, and if you are, your life is probably out of control. I'm still not sure about the market for this kind of book."

"It's not a black-or-white problem," I said. "These are everyday addicts, people who still function and work and shop where we work and shop. People like you and me."

"I'm surprised we're struggling so much with this concept," said Donna. "Of course there are everyday addictions. I'll admit that I'm an Internet junkie, and my husband would be smiling if he were here listening to this conversation. It's not a joke, though I've got to admit I've never thought of it as an addiction."

"You're slowly coming out of denial," I said smiling. "This is good. We're making progress in our group therapy session today."

Everyone laughed.

"I think I'm beginning to understand," Kirk added. "However, I'm still not sure people want to hear this message."

"Of course they don't want to hear the message," I said. "That's precisely why we're obligated to send it. Someone has to come out of denial long enough to consider the possibility that we've all got addictive traits and symptoms. Many of us are card-carrying addicts even though we go to church every week and hold down full-time jobs. We're addicted to everyday things like coffee, cell phones, Coke, and shopping."

By now, the team was starting to get it: Everyday addicts are everywhere, and we shouldn't be too quick to exclude ourselves.

"This is also the perfect opportunity," I continued, "to show people how everyday addictions, habits, and compulsions hamper our freedom to be all that God wants us to be. That's really the point of the book. Addictions nail us to our particular drug of choice and limit our freedom. God brings freedom to our lives."

"You know," Kirk said thoughtfully, "the more I think about this, the more excited I get. Christians need to be talking about addictions. We have answers to issues of addiction and bondage. We have power from our relationship in Christ—true freedom."

"Yes," I said, "and I want to offer hope and help to the hard-core addict, the soft-core addict, and the everyday addict. I want to bring our faith to bear on these issues."

Perhaps you can relate. You go to work every day. You've got kids and a home, and you hold down a full-time job. Yet you struggle with compulsive behaviors common to many others. That's why this book is for you. Together we'll learn about addictions—we'll talk about something most of us try to avoid. And we'll discover answers and see what Scripture has to say on the matter.

In the Next Pew

Picture yourself in a church. The sanctuary is full. Standing in front of a 300-member church, I give the following instructions:

"I want everyone to stand and close your eyes. I'm going to list a number of common problems. Sit down if one rings true for you.

"If you've struggled with compulsive eating, anorexia, bulimia, the use of laxatives for weight loss, or excessive fears about body image, please sit down.

"Anyone who's struggled with compulsive drinking, illicit substances, or overuse of prescription medications, please sit down.

"If you've struggled with compulsive gambling, spending, or shopping, please sit down. That includes compulsive garage sale and e-Bay shopping." Nervous giggles are heard as more people sit down.

"Anyone who's struggled with sexual addiction, including serial affairs, serial dating, pornography, or compulsive masturbation, please sit down.

"Everyone who's struggled with work addiction, please sit down. This includes compulsively checking your e-mail, obsessively scanning the Internet for your favorite daily blog, and issues with power and control at work.

"Anyone who's struggled with compulsive television or movie viewing, please sit down.

"Everyone who's struggled with compulsive exercise addiction or competition addiction, please sit down.

"If you've struggled from the ravages of seeking approval from others, please sit down. This includes problems with codependency."

The remaining 12 people were noticeably anxious, shifting positions and fidgeting. They had their eyes closed, but they'd heard their fellow worshippers dropping out in droves. Now they wondered whether they were addiction free or if I was ready to point one out that fit them.

"Now, those who struggle with compulsive worry, perfectionism, and religious addictions, please sit down."

"Okay," I say. "Open your eyes."

Someone yells out, "I can't believe it!"

One man and one woman are still standing.

"Those still standing, please sit down," I say. "We don't know everyone's story, but what is clearly apparent is that the vast majority of us face common, everyday addictions. We're all in this boat together. Thankfully, we can experience freedom from addictions, and the first powerful step is coming out of the silent and secretive shadows of shame and into the light of grace, surrender, and acceptance."

The Conspiracy of Silence

I've always wanted to conduct this kind of exercise. I believe it would do much to end the shame we have about our compulsive and addictive behaviors. What relief people would feel as they looked around and realized that everyone struggles with some addiction or compulsion. What a relief to know and admit that all of us are flawed and in need of God's grace and tender care as well as the care of a supportive group of people who are struggling with the same issues.

But what about our imaginary scene of those two people left standing? Were they really free from addictive or compulsive thinking or behavior? I doubt it. I suspect they were caught in the throes of denial (Don't Even Notice I Am Lying). For many people, coming clean with their problems is difficult. Many in our world won't jump on the bandwagon to admit their problems, but this need not stop us from being open and honest about our problems.

We're caught up in an amazing conspiracy of silence. We want to see the world neatly divided into those with addictions and those without. We don't acknowledge that those who claim to be free from addictions merely appear normal and refuse to talk about their addictive and compulsive behaviors. This leaves them to suffer alone in shame. It also focuses even more attention on those who clearly struggle with addictions. This dichotomy is completely false. If we are honest, willing to shed the heavy cloak of denial, we notice addicts everywhere—even in our own home.

Only in recent years have we begun to offer legitimate treatment for some of the obvious addictions, such as alcohol and drug abuse. We even endorse such programs in our churches. However, we still don't recognize the myriad other addictions, let alone help people deal with them.

Defining Addiction

The bottom line is that we're all addicted to something. Although we have been taught to think of *addict* as a dirty word, it is an apt description for all of us relatively normal people.

Let's consider several aspects of everyday addictions.

First, an addiction is a compulsive physical and psychological dependence on habit-forming substances, like nicotine, alcohol, or drugs, or on processes, such as shopping, eating, or sex. The substances give us a physiological high. Meanwhile, "process addictions," where we engage compulsively in activities such as gambling, viewing pornography, video gaming, or shopping, also change our mood.

Second, we continue to engage in these mood-altering activities in spite of obvious negative consequences. We know that smoking is bad for our health, but we can't seem to stop. We know that staying at the slot machines well past our determined curfew or beyond our self-imposed spending limit is destructive, but we can't seem to pull ourselves away. We know that eating more than we need is detrimental to our health, but that doesn't stop us.

Third, we often need more and more of the substance or behavior to get the desired high. In other words, our tolerance increases. We continue eating well beyond satiation. We spend more than we can afford, hoping to regain a good feeling. We continue to gamble in order to win back what we have lost or to hit "the big one." We continue to drink until we literally cannot drink any more. And the more we drink, the more we need to drink to gain the desired effect.

Fourth, we lie about and deny our behavior because we are ashamed. Inside, we know our lives are out of control. We know someone will be displeased with our actions, and so, in an attempt to avoid negative consequences, we lie about them. We hide our alcohol use from others; we hide the new clothes we purchased and tell our mates that we bought them months ago; we are dishonest about our frequency of gambling and the losses we've incurred; we're dishonest about the hours we spend working. This deception, of course, only compounds our problems.

Finally, we allow our lives to become unmanageable. At some point the wheels fall off the cart. Our mates say they can no longer tolerate our drinking. Our bosses fire us because of our repeated failure to get work done on time after the late-night poker parties. We hide in shame because of the 50 extra pounds we carry. We're so tied to our cell phones that we begin to annoy our spouse, our friends, and even ourselves. We're out of control. We've given up the power of our lives to a substance or behavior. We've lost our ability to make healthy choices.

Anesthetized

Having lost control of your life, you're still stuck in denial. You still believe you can fly under the radar. You still have your job, your spouse, your home, your bank account, and your faith. You're feeling a bit smug because you believe you're still in complete control of your life. You're certain you would have been one of those left standing when the roll was called.

Not so fast.

Is it possible that addiction and compulsion have struck your life as well, but you've anesthetized yourself so you don't feel the pain? Are you vaguely aware of feeling distanced from others because of your particular compulsion or addiction? Do you feel stifled in your personal and spiritual growth? Do you feel hidden shame and guilt? Might you be harboring hidden problems you've never called addictions?

Consider these common scenarios:

Sheryl has had yo-yo weight problems her entire life. Now 40, she's tried every gimmick diet and attended countless weight-loss programs, but she exceeds her ideal weight by 75 pounds. She's learned to accommodate her problem. Although she hates being heavy, she's rationalized the problem and works overtime to tell herself that she must be comfortable in her own skin. She's anesthetized herself to the pain of her eating addiction and continues to gain more weight each year. Her health is in jeopardy, her self-esteem has been damaged, and her marriage suffers. Still, she's quit calling her weight a problem because admitting the truth simply causes too much pain.

Jed is a 30-year-old workaholic, a Microsoft engineer who averages 60 hours a week. Like many of his coworkers, he carries a "CrackBerry" (BlackBerry) on his hip as a badge of admission into the hardworking, upwardly mobile society. He's well-rewarded for his work and rarely thinks about the hours he puts in. His wife works equally hard as a financial analyst, and only rarely does either of them mention the possibility of slowing down. They have silently agreed not to talk about their problem. They're anesthetized to the pain that comes from having too little time for friendships, leisure activities, and quality time with their children. They're tired and irritable, and the luster is wearing off their marriage—but still they continue to push forward as if nothing were wrong.

Carl is a gambler. He can be found nightly at a local casino. He insists that he rarely spends more than what he can afford, though he acknowledges that he hides the true amount of his losses from his wife. She doesn't confront him. In fact, she often joins him. Both are in their late forties and know their retirement monies are paying for blackjack and slots, but neither wants to change. Their working lives are boring, their marriage is boring, and the casino offers them a respite from the pain. They've anesthetized themselves to the problem by denying that it exists.

Kathy is a 35-year-old mother of three who spends much of her time worrying about her depressed mother. Her mother calls her daily and complains about her life. The oldest of four children, Kathy has always been "the responsible one." She knows she cannot "fix" her mother, but she feels compelled to keep trying, to the detriment of her own well-being. She alternates between feeling exhausted, angry, hurt, sad, and discouraged when obsessing about her mother. Secretly, she also feels powerful, needed, and important when attempting to control her mother's moods. She's addicted to this codependent and destructive relationship.

I could go on, telling story after story of addictive and compulsive behavior that hasn't yet reached a crisis point. This parade of addictions is with us every day in every walk of life. We anesthetize our pain with our substance or behavior of choice, secretly hoping we'll never have to face the power of our problems.

A Parade of Addictions

In case I haven't convinced you yet that we're a parade of addicts, let's make a list of everyday addictions. Let's take a look at the activities and substances that can hook us. Let's look at the ways we can lose our souls to the powers of these addictions, relinquishing our ability to choose what is best for us along the way. Here are some everyday addictions:

> drugs, alcohol, and gambling
> food, caffeine, and sugar

sex and pornography

work and perfectionism

codependency, approval, and worry

spending, shopping, and coupon-clipping

television, video, and video-gaming

exercise and sports

love, romance, and romance novels

money, accumulation, and success

religion

e-mail, Internet, and chat rooms

cell phones

power and anger

The list could go on and on. I suspect you have recognized my point: Virtually anything can become a compulsion and qualify as an everyday addiction.

Humans are prone to addiction and compulsive behaviors. What begins as a benign activity, such as buying something on the Internet, can gradually become addictive. For some people, innocuous and infrequent spending soon becomes obsessive—they do it more and more, hiding their behaviors from others. For others, random outings to the casino become an infatuation with the neon lights and the glimmer of winning something big. They move from infrequent outings to an obsessive attachment to the activity, cloaking their behavior in secrecy and denial. For others, the occasional dinner party and single glass of wine slips easily into two or three glasses of wine nightly. Soon they're hooked!

Society as Addict

Why can we so easily be hooked? Why are we self-controlled in one area of our lives and completely unable to set limits in another? Anne Wilson Schaef has an interesting perspective on the matter. Schaef, author of *When Society Becomes an Addict,* says the addictions we can see are only the tip of the iceberg and that society itself reinforces addictions by ignoring their presence. She believes that no one has only one addiction. Instead, we all have multiple addictions, characterized by self-centeredness, dishonesty, preoccupation with control, abnormal thinking processes, repressed feelings, and ethical deterioration. She asserts that our society not only encourages addictions but sees them as normal. As someone recovers from one addiction, another is likely to surface.

Is this why we smile when we mention addiction to caffeine, nicotine, food, cell phones, and e-mail? Schaef's theory makes sense. Few people are screaming about the rampant obesity in our society. Few are carping about our addictive interest in television, movies, or movie stars, or the tremendous negative influence these have on us. Few even decry the moral deterioration caused by pornography. Like television and the movies, these are considered "victimless" problems.

Everyday addictions, however, are not innocuous problems. Though they are everyday, they bring serious trouble. They are addictions, whether large or small, accepted or treated with contempt. The excuse that "the rest of society is doing it" doesn't make a behavior less harmful.

This is serious stuff that affects each of us. It may not be pleasant to talk about, but the truth will set us free.

No Longer Choosing

Addictions are particularly debilitating because they undermine our power to choose. Although we certainly make the decision to take the first drag on a cigarette and perhaps even the second or third, we quickly become hooked.

We choose to pull the first lever of the slot machine, but very quickly those "one-arm bandits" are choosing us. Our choice becomes a compulsion, and we can't say no.

For years we've considered the addict weak willed, as though he belongs to some lower class. Meanwhile, those from the upper class who succumb to an addiction have been whisked away to some posh, private facility for rehab. We still maintain a similar view of addictions. We believe we cannot become addicted if we are spiritual enough, powerful enough, strong enough, or smart enough. With enough willpower, we will be safe.

Wrong. It's *not* a matter of willpower. You have willpower to not take the first drink, the first puff on a cigarette, or your first peek at pornography. But once you take that first step, choice quickly begins to disappear.

Because we believe that only the weak become addicted, we naively think we can dabble with substances and other activities without getting hooked. Listen to the words of one man who shared his situation with me recently.

"I couldn't believe how quickly I got hooked on pornography. One day an image popped up on my computer. No one was home, and I looked at it for a while. Once I viewed it, I was aroused and hit on some links to other sites. I'm not even sure how it happened, but within weeks I was racing home in the middle of the day to spend time on pornographic websites. I'd still be doing it today if my wife hadn't caught me. I feel humiliated and embarrassed, not to mention the fact that my productivity at work began to decline."

Not surprisingly, his wife was furious with him. She accused him of being sick, weak willed, and twisted. But he was actually none of the above. He was addicted, that's all. Not weak willed, not twisted, not sick. Addicted.

Some people will surely accuse me of letting this man off the hook. But I'm not letting him off the hook—he's clearly on it. He's hooked all right, by his addiction. Some people will continue to label him, but he and I know he is a good man with morals, values, and strong convictions. He simply gave in to temptation and then, because of his makeup, became addicted.

The Pleasure Principle

Sigmund Freud discovered another important principle that is absolutely apropos to our discussion on addictions. Freud said that we are all inclined to seek immediate gratification through pleasure and to avoid pain. Scott Peck, in his book *The Road Less Traveled,* talks about avoiding problems:

> Fearing the pain involved, almost all of us, to a greater or lesser degree, attempt to avoid problems. We procrastinate, hoping they will go away. We ignore them, forget them, pretend they do not exist. We even take drugs to assist us in ignoring them, so that by deadening ourselves to the pain we can forget the problems that cause the pain. We attempt to skirt around problems rather than meet them head on.[1]

Seeking pleasure and avoiding pain is nothing new. Solomon wrote about the meaninglessness of pleasures:

> And what does pleasure accomplish? I tried cheering myself with wine, and embracing folly—my mind still guiding me with wisdom. I wanted to see what was worthwhile for men to do under heaven during the few days of their lives...I denied myself nothing my eyes desired; I refused my heart no pleasure...Yet when I surveyed all that my hands had done and what I had toiled to achieve, everything was meaningless, a chasing after the wind; nothing was gained under the sun (Ecclesiastes 2:2-3,10-11).

The wisest man of his time tells us that seeking pleasure is common—and, in many ways, fruitless. We seek it, but it does not give us what we ultimately need, which is to find our purpose and meaning in God. It is a temporary relief from pain.

We all want to avoid pain, and seeking relief from our everyday struggles leads to our everyday addictions. Seeking relief from our problems leads us to the very substances and activities that alter our brain chemistry and have us running back for more regardless of the negative consequences.

Brain Damaged

I'm being serious when I say that we're all brain damaged.

Addictions have been clearly linked to certain chemicals released in the brain, thus leading us to seek certain forms of relief again and again. Because we're all part of the mass of everyday addicts, we're all, by definition, a bit brain damaged.

An illicit drug is taken the first time by choice to relieve depression or stress or for recreational purposes. We become involved in an activity because it is enjoyable. Soon, however, our ability to choose is weakened. Why? Because repeated drug use or certain repetitive and compulsive activities disrupt well-balanced systems in the brain. Repeated use of marijuana, cocaine, or alcohol causes a surge in levels of a brain chemical called dopamine, resulting in a feeling of pleasure. (And remember, we're all suckers for pleasure.) The brain remembers this feeling of pleasure and wants to repeat it, thus creating a dependency that can soon become an addiction.

Brain researchers have discovered that particular activities can trigger the release of our own feel-good drugs called endorphins. Although these natural pain-relieving neurotransmitters make us feel good, we can also become addicted to them. Thus, when addicted gamblers or shoppers are satisfying their cravings, endorphins are produced and released within the brain, creating a high and reinforcing the people's positive associations with the activity. As with illicit drugs, consistently engaging in addictive activities is also believed to cause excessive stimulation and leads eventually to tolerance and dependence.

Addictive substances and behaviors also affect regions of the brain that help us control our desires and emotions. The resulting lack of control leads addicted people to compulsively pursue substances or activities even when these substances or behaviors are no longer intrinsically rewarding.

Gerald May, in his wonderful book *Addiction and Grace,* helps us understand how all of this applies to our commonplace, everyday addictions. "The same kind of cellular dynamics apply to nonsubstance addictions. If we had been talking about addiction to money, power, images of ourselves or of God, we could have said much the same about what happens to our nerve cells."[2]

May goes on to offer us a very practical example of how little habits can become addictive.

> Consider a very minor addiction, one that seems to harbor no special destructiveness. Let us say that I have established a routine of having a cup of coffee and reading the paper before starting the day. I enjoy the quiet, undemanding quality of this time and would be loathe to call it an addiction. But, I have been engaging in this little routine for years, and the cells of my brain have become adapted to it. They are used to the whole sequence of the time: the gentle slowness of waking up, the familiarity of my favorite chair, the gradual stimulation of the reading, the friendly jolt of the coffee's caffeine playing out its own little addiction fix, the sounds of the house waking up all around me. All the countless sensations and behaviors of this time become mutually associated in patterned sequences of synapses, with billions of cells having become adapted to certain amounts of neurotransmitters in certain ways at certain times.[3]

Were this pattern to become disrupted, May would feel the irritability and shakiness associated with withdrawal symptoms. Although his symptoms would be far less severe than those of alcoholics coming off binges or drug addicts coming down from their drug of choice, a vast number of brain cells would still be involved.

Such is also the case for our everyday addictions. We feel out of sorts when we lose our cell phone or are unable to check our e-mail for a few days or perhaps even a few hours. We feel disconcerted if we cannot indulge in our nightly glass of wine or weekend shopping trip. We're uncomfortable if our television goes on the blink and we're left having to converse with one another.

The Truth Will Set You Free

Jesus said, "You will know the truth, and the truth will set you free" (John 8:32). Just before saying this, however, He said, "If you hold to my teaching, you are really my disciples." Jesus connects freedom to being disciples. He offers a path out of the bondage of addictions—the path of discipleship.

We know this principle, yet we remain reluctant truth seekers. We remain unwilling disciples, choosing instead to believe that we can find our own way out of the wilderness. We've gone hundreds of years without openly talking about addiction—the proverbial elephant in the room. Why talk about it now? Haven't we been doing just fine letting the beast roam freely as long as it's not affecting anyone? Haven't we done fine on our own?

Let's get this straight: Elephants don't roam freely without affecting people. They poop; they smell; they bump into things, crowd our living spaces, and generally wreak havoc. In future chapters, we'll talk about the effect the elephant in the room has on our ability to function. Furthermore, we are not doing so well winging it on our own. We're employing massive denial when we claim that elephants are nothing more than a nuisance and that we can manage our lives just fine, thank you.

Why talk about it now? Because we've been introduced to concepts such as codependency and boundaries and have a hunch that the problem is larger than we believed, so perhaps we're ready to hear more about it.

We're also developing addictions at faster and faster rates. Methamphetamine abuse has exploded in recent years, as have e-mail, cell phone, and Internet addictions. You can almost hear the clanging of balls and chains as we meander through life. We're not free—we live in an addicted society, and our addictions are increasing.

Finally, we're talking about it now because it's time to break free from everyday addictions. It's time to look in the mirror and determine whether we've become enslaved to some addictive substance or activity. Whether your everyday addiction is debilitating methamphetamine abuse or a more socially acceptable addiction to e-mail, these behaviors and substances have the power to enslave us.

As we travel together through this book, I invite you to consider the possibility that all of us are encumbered with everyday addictions that control us. All of us desperately need freedom from substances or activities that restrict us to a particular way of behaving. We yearn for a free life.

Addiction Does Not Discriminate

Addiction doesn't just happen to the derelict. Addiction is not simply a problem for the emaciated heroin addict. Addiction isn't relegated to back alleys.

We have to understand that we have found the addict, and the addict is us. You and me. Our mothers, fathers, sisters, and brothers. Our best friends and our worst enemies. Everyday addictions are commonplace, testing the rich and famous as well as the middle-class suburbanites. Everyday addictions attack those who are poor in faith and rich in faith.

The truth of the matter is that no one is a cookie-cutter addict—we come in all sizes and shapes. We're a mishmash of cocaine addicts, cell phone addicts, food addicts, and gambling addicts. We overspend, overwork, shop too much, and become entangled in sexual sins. We're addicted to innumerable drugs and activities that create a wide range of everyday addicts.

So we have many different kinds of addicts, and many are

Christians. They come in all faiths, ages, shapes, sizes, and economic backgrounds. We'd like to think we're insulated from these problems, but this simply isn't true. In fact, as many addicts are inside the church as outside.

I'm pushing for us to get comfortable with the notion. The first step is to nod your head and sit down!

CHAPTER TWO

Distant Elephants

We should know that too much of anything, even a good thing, may prove to be our undoing. We need...to set definite boundaries on our appetites.

WILLIAM J. BENNETT

NEON LIGHTS, FLASHY BILLBOARDS, enticing commercials...bigger and fancier casinos are cropping up all across Washington State. Each new casino appears larger, brighter, and gaudier than the last. Amenities include huge parking lots, luxury hotels, celebrity head-liners, endless rows of slot machines, and ingenious ways to gamble. All this for crowds that seem to grow by the day.

I was in a casino recently. At a loss for a place to watch a base-ball playoff game, I suspected the casino would feature it on a huge screen and offer cheap appetizers, the perfect combination for a big-time sporting event.

When I walked through the large entry, complete with doormen, I was stunned by the plush carpeting, sparkling chandeliers, and huge, colorful paintings on the wall. I thought perhaps I had taken a wrong turn and was in the Waldorf-Astoria in New York City. This casino had no dim hallways or dark, smoky rooms. The furnishings were luxurious. Gambling was clearly big business.

I found my big-screen television and enjoyed the game, but I couldn't help but wonder about the people hovering over the gaming tables and sitting on bar stools at the blackjack tables. It was Sunday afternoon, yet hundreds of people were spending a bundle on their addiction.

When I got home I told my wife what I'd seen. "Is there really that great of a demand for these things?" I asked.

"Apparently so," Christie replied.

I've begun to take notice of the activity at casinos I pass. The parking lots are filled, and limo and bus service are provided to those who need a lift. One casino not far from my home has an espresso kiosk, a gas station, a convenience store, and a parking garage.

If you want to gamble, you can rest assured that that within 50 miles of your home you're likely to run into a monument of flashing lights and promises of financial independence.

I'm still surprised that so few people are talking about this phenomenon. I might hear people say they went to a casino for a cheap meal, but I never hear anyone address the growing problems with gambling addictions. I hear plenty about the latest $10 million lottery drawing but nothing about services for those who are addicted.

Obtaining accurate information about gambling addiction is difficult, but gambling is growing at phenomenal rates and has become a high-profile, socially accepted activity. According to information Greg Jantz compiled in his book *Turning the Tables on Gambling*, 37 states now have lotteries. From 1973 to 1997, state lotteries grew from $2 billion in sales to $34 billion. Fifteen million people display some kind of gambling addiction. Still, with its larger and larger profile, we don't talk about it.[1]

Psychologists call this phenomenon *distant elephants.* Here's how it goes: On the rare occasion when we sit down and talk seriously about this societal phenomenon or when we fully acknowledge that we are raising a new generation of addicts, we talk as if the problem were out there, on some distant horizon, like distant elephants. The elephants aren't here, stinking up our living rooms, creating havoc in our homes and marriages. They're out there, somewhere. Perhaps you can relate.

The phenomenon of collectively ignoring a serious problem is called *collusion*—and this is something we all do in response to many different kinds of problems. Gambling is only one of many addictions we'll address in this book. Although I'm not particularly political, I presume that at least part of our collusion stems from the fact that these same casinos bring in a boatload of tourism revenue for counties. Therefore, we wink at these monoliths. Except for the occasional stink, we could completely ignore the odor of these not-so-distant elephants.

Later

At least to some extent, we're all guilty of minimizing our particular addictions, whether yours happens to be a food addiction or a shopping addiction, or whether you, like me, can wink when it comes to caffeine, work, and accumulation addictions. I'll deal with those things later, I insist. No one is confronting me, and I tell myself I'm not hurting anyone, so I procrastinate rather than face my addictions.

Who hasn't had these thoughts?

- *I'll work on limiting my shopping—later.*
- *I'll limit my bingo playing—later.*
- *I'll cut back on work—later.*
- *I'll find more time to spend with my family—later.*

- *I'll reduce my drinking—later.*
- *I'll go on that diet and join the gym—later.*
- *I'll quit using marijuana—later.*
- *I'll stop surfing the Internet for pornography—later.*

And the list goes on. We postpone the inevitable because facing our addictions is uncomfortable. This is because dealing with them means acknowledging the feelings we've submerged beneath our addictive behavior. It means facing the symptoms of withdrawal we'll feel if we give up our addictions. It means bringing the problem "up close and personal" as opposed to holding it at arm's length.

In fact, we are loath to call these problems addictions. We're much more comfortable labeling them as mistakes, poor judgment, or even character flaws. We use any number of disguises to avoid calling the problem what it is—an addiction.

But this postponement is at the heart of the distant-elephant phenomenon and assumes that the problems are out there (as opposed to within us). We insist we'll deal with them later. Later, of course, never comes.

Later is one way we anesthetize ourselves from the harshness of the problems. *Later* is one way we convince ourselves the problems aren't that bad. *Later* allows me to drive by the magnificent casino on my way home every night and hardly give it a second thought—except for whether or not I'll be able to watch this Sunday afternoon's NFL game there.

Collusion

For *later* to work, however, we must agree that we're going to ignore these problems for now. It is one thing for me to ignore my personal history of work addiction, which took incredible denial on my part, but quite another for an entire society to collude together to ignore our entire country's work addiction. Corporations push for more work, more efficiency, and more hours, and only recently have many people given notice to the debilitating impact this all has on the family and even on production.

For an individual to ignore his obesity is one thing, but for a nation to ignore its addiction to fast food and overeating is quite another. Corporations make incredible profits off our tendencies for fast food while statistics are clear about the negative impact obesity has on health. Excessive weight puts us at immense risk for heart attacks, diabetes, and other related illness.

We decry government spending, but we personally rack up more and more debt, paying huge interest rates on credit cards. We're bombarded with opportunities for more credit, even while we drown under the debt we're already carrying.

Consider the enormous energy we spend to act as if these problems don't exist. We pretend something destructive is not occurring, but we honestly know it is. Although we may believe we can ignore them without consequences, we'll explore together the incredible emotional and physical cost of this collusion and these addictions in later chapters.

Nora Ephron, in the opening words of her humorous memoir *I Feel Bad About My Neck,* offers a delightful discourse about collusion.

> I feel bad about my neck. Truly I do. If you saw my neck, you might feel bad about it too, but you'd probably be too polite to let on. If I said something to you on the subject—something like "I absolutely cannot stand my neck"—you'd undoubtedly respond by saying something nice, like "I don't know what you're talking about." You'd be lying, of course, but I forgive you. I tell lies like that all the time.[2]

What is not funny about Ephron's anecdote is that we can imagine having the exact same kind of discussion with someone about alcohol, food, or sex. If you brought up your problem to me, I would likely comfort and dismiss you or desperately try to change the subject. It's too personal, too uncomfortable, and it leaves me vulnerable to having the same conversation about secret sins and vulnerabilities in my life.

I'm currently working with a couple in their forties. The woman, Victoria, is at least 100 pounds overweight. At her age and with her lack of exercise, her obesity has created numerous health risks.

Ken and Victoria came to see me not because of her obesity, but because of Ken's drinking. I learned that he has abused alcohol through most of their 20-year marriage. Victoria has left him several times after he broke promises to stay sober.

A stocky, engaging man who works for the U.S. Postal Service, Ken envisions retirement sometime in the next ten years. He is a strong Christian and has made attempts to work on his alcoholism, but he has never dedicated himself fully to remaining sober. He has taken half measures, and his alcoholism is more advanced than it was years ago. His rheumy eyes and irritable, depressed demeanor are outward signs of inward degeneration. His addiction is advancing as he requires more beer now than ever before to get his desired buzz.

Victoria has become bitter about Ken's alcoholism. She has periodically demanded that he move out, and that motivated him to deal with his addiction—for two or three months at a time. He'd go to a program and quit drinking, and she'd invite him back into the home. A short time later, he'd begin drinking again—slowly at first, but then picking up momentum until he was right back where he started.

When they came to see me, Victoria had again asked Ken to leave the home and deal with his addiction. Although reluctant to leave, he faced his situation with integrity. He immersed himself in the New Beginnings recovery program at their church.

Not long after they began seeing me, Ken intimated that he wanted to use counseling to talk about other problems besides his drinking.

"How are you?" I asked Ken as he sat down in my office for the individual appointment we'd scheduled.

"Well," he said slowly, "I'm not sure how to begin. This has never been easy for me."

"What has never been easy?"

"Sharing the things that bug me in my marriage," he continued. "The focus has always been on my drinking, and maybe rightly so. But anytime I want to talk about other concerns, I get shut down. So I don't talk about them. Instead, I go out to the garage and drink. I think it's time to talk about my concerns as well as Victoria's."

"That makes sense," I said. "Are you saying that you don't think Victoria wants to hear your concerns?"

"It's not that simple," he said. "I don't know that she'd stop me from talking. But if it gets too personal—and this does—then I get the feeling that I'd better keep things to myself. To be fair, she's done that with my drinking. We're pretty good at ignoring our problems."

"Could you explain that for me?"

"Don't get me wrong," he said. "I'm not blaming my drinking on Victoria. But she's never been very consistent in dealing with it. For a while she's on me, and then she kind of ignores it. And I'm the same way with her weight. You've got to believe that it bugs me to pieces. She tires easily and doesn't want to hike anymore. She doesn't turn me on the way she used to, and our intimacy has really been affected. But how do you tell your wife she's fat, especially when she's made it perfectly clear that it's her problem and none of my business?"

Ken stared at me, obviously frustrated.

"So here I am," he continued, "out on my ear, living in my buddy's spare bedroom, addressing my problem but still not addressing hers."

"This is probably as good a time as ever to get all the issues out on the table."

"She's not going to like it, I can tell you that. We have this unspoken agreement to ignore my drinking and *never* to talk about her weight. And we haven't even come close to dealing with spending. It scares me to even think about opening the door to that subject."

The more Ken and I talked, the more I realized they had multiple addictions, layered one on top of the other. To compound the problem, they were partners in collusion—they tacitly reached an agreement not to talk about certain issues. If Ken and Victoria were to have an honest and authentic relationship, they would need to agree that every issue was fair game to be brought to the table. In fact, it was critical to the health of their relationship that they learn to name every elephant parading through their living room.

Mass Collusion

Just as Ken and Victoria can collude to ignore his drinking and her eating, entire households, communities, and nations can wink at addictive behavior. We don't want to see the truth, for if we did, we'd have to face the consequences of our choices.

The apostle Paul dealt directly with muddling the truth. Speaking to Timothy, he said, "the time will come when men will not put up with sound doctrine. Instead, to suit their own desires, they will gather around them a great number of teachers to say what their itching ears want to hear. They will turn their ears away from the truth and turn aside to myths" (2 Timothy 4:3-4).

Sometimes it seems to me that we are all fish in a giant fishbowl and cannot see the water. We're looking out, and at times we can clearly see things and issues outside. But looking inside, at our own behavior, we are like fish looking for the water. It's all too close, and our defenses are simply too much to overcome.

I had lunch yesterday with Gregg, a friend from church. A middle-aged man with a bright, eager smile, he'd waved at me when I saw him in town and invited me to lunch. For an hour and a half we talked about life—his story, my story, our story. In many places, his struggles overlapped mine. Over a bowl of mushroom and lentil soup, on a crisp November afternoon, we were honest with one another.

Gregg's candor was disarming. He didn't try to paint his life in pretty colors with fancy words and idealized images. His language was raw, transparent. We spoke of broken marriages, distant relationships to his kids, business failures, regrets, and losses. We recognized this transparency and shared how freeing it was not to posture with one another. We're both old enough to know that doing so would have been disingenuous. There was no need to pretend or collude with one another about life.

But even as we shared our stories, I could feel the tension building within me. How honest should I really be with Gregg? How much should I reveal? For a few moments I fought my urge to posture, to pretend to be someone other than who I am.

Straightforward conversations are rare in my line of work. Too often a person attempts to sell me a story about the magnificence of his life even though both of us know it's not true. He wants to collude with me, pretending that everything is fine, but we both know that it's not. Sometimes I give in to the collusion, and sometimes I don't. Sometimes I smile and wink, knowing that one or both of us simply can't handle the intensity of the truth at that moment.

Blind Spots

The incongruity of our actions is all around us. Just today, while listening to the local sports radio station, I heard a poignant advertisement for an inpatient alcohol treatment program that was presented in a most unusual context.

"Are you tired of going to weekly meetings, only to have cravings all the time? Are you sick and tired of being sick and tired? Give us a weekend, and we'll give you back your home, your wife, your family, and your life," the spokesman said. "I've been there, and I owe my life to this program."

Good for them, I thought. Here was a message people needed to hear. But before I had finished applauding the station's willingness to promote alcohol treatment, the DJs began laughing about the "toot" they'd been on the night before.

"Wasn't that a great party?" one said.

"The booze was really flowing, that's for sure," the other replied.

"You did pretty well, from what I remember," the first said.

"Just trying to keep up with you, my friend."

Innocent repartee? I don't think so. For several minutes I felt like I was listening to a couple of boys at the bar. Just guys out having fun—except the station had obviously purchased an ad noting the very dangers these men were laughing about. I wondered if either the station manager or the client recognized that these ads were completely negated by the DJs' informal endorsement of booze.

Blind spots. Collusion. Serious problems lost in the muddle of truth.

Good Intentions

When you think about it, it's amazing that all manner of addictions flourish and new ones continue to crop up, even while we admit these same addictions are killers. We know that addictions kill the soul, the spirit, and in many cases, the body of the afflicted. None of us would be so brazen as to suggest that eating disorders, including obesity, anorexia, and bulimia, are not hazardous. But at the same time we wink when it comes to having a serious conversation about them. Why is that?

In May of 2006, HBO, *USA Today,* and Gallup conducted a survey among U.S. adults who have an immediate family member who has had a drug or alcohol addiction. Here are some of their key findings:

- Three-quarters of the family members think addiction is a disease.
- Three-quarters think people who are addicted to drugs can make a complete recovery from their addiction.

- Eight out of ten think alcoholics can make a complete recovery from their addiction.

- Over eight out of ten think alcoholics must totally abstain from alcohol to recover from their addiction.

- Only a third of the family members think that medications that can treat alcoholism are available.

- The effects of a family member's addiction are usually described as *emotional, devastating,* and *horrible.*

- Almost half say they have felt a sense of shame about their family member's addiction.

- Seven out of ten say that a family member's addiction has had a major or minor effect on their emotional or mental health.

- Almost one out of ten of those who say a family member's addiction has had a major negative impact on their financial situation say they have had to take out a loan or run up credit card bills as a direct result of this addiction.

- About a fifth of those who say a family member's addiction has had a major negative impact on their marriage, family relationships, or emotional health say they sought professional counseling.

- Half say this addiction has brought their family closer, but a third feel it has pushed them apart.

- One-third say the addiction has caused estrangement among family members.

- Just over half say the addicted family member has admitted his or her addiction to them, and just under half say the addicted person has not.

- Seven out of ten say they have personally confronted the family member about the addiction.

- Four out of ten say their family member has overcome

the addiction. One out of ten think their family member wants to recover, but almost a fifth believe they do not.

- Almost half say their family member has never sought treatment. Of those whose family member has sought treatment, three out of ten sought treatment only after intervention.

- Eight out of ten say they have some idea on how to find treatment for their family member's addiction.

- More than half of the respondents whose family member sought treatment say the family member had to repeat treatment.

- Almost four out of ten of the respondents whose family member sought treatment say their family member completely recovered, but about six out of ten say their family member either showed no improvement or got better but did not completely recover.

- Of those whose family member sought treatment, almost half say the family member relapsed and almost one out of ten say there was no improvement at all.

- Family support or pressure was most often cited as the primary reason the family member was able to overcome addiction.

- Three quarters of the respondents say their family member was addicted to alcohol. The remaining quarter of the addictions were to a variety of drugs.

These are, of course, statistics on drug and alcohol abuse. Statistics on gambling, online gaming, pornography, and myriad other addictions are harder to find. We know, however, that all addictions kill.

Jeff and Debra Jay, in their book *Love First*, tell us that good intentions are partly to blame for our minimization of problems. In talking specifically about alcoholism, they point the finger at families for enabling the very behaviors they despise.

Almost all families inadvertently enable addicted loved ones by helping them avoid the negative consequences of addiction. For alcoholics and addicts to stay comfortable in their addiction, they need the help of the very people who want them to stop drinking. Family, friends, and co-workers are uninformed recruits, who unknowingly enable the addiction. Every alcoholic and addict has an enabling network or collection of people, professionals, or institutions whose combined efforts unwittingly allow addiction to continue flourishing in the addict's life.[3]

How can that be? Are we really aiding and abetting those we love in their self-abusive habits and addictions? These authors say we are—and I agree. We do so with good intentions. We aren't trying to hurt those we love. In fact, we are usually motivated by our concern for them. We have good intentions but are afraid to step up and tell the truth. Consider this list of good intentions gone awry.

- putting out sweets and candy for the obese family member
- going shopping with the friend whose credit cards are maxed out
- watching television with the TV addict
- laughing at the antics of the alcoholic friend who's had too much to drink
- ignoring your mate's addiction to pornography
- forgiving your mate's sexual indiscretion—again
- creating or embracing excuses for someone's drug abuse

You know the routine. We make an unspoken pact with friends and family. "You don't call me on my stuff, and I won't call you on yours." We even have a way to spiritualize our collusion—"I won't point out the speck in your eye, and you won't point out the plank in mine."

Maybe we have good intentions, or maybe we're just afraid to talk about the emperor who isn't wearing any clothes. Either way, we choose to dance around the truth.

Deceived

Collusion is actually a form of deception. We know casinos are being built at alarming rates; we know that gambling is proliferating; we know that gambling addiction ruins marriages, families, and souls. But if we agree to look the other way while we cite the many pluses that come from the millions of dollars in tourism and lottery revenues, perhaps we're not really deceiving ourselves. And so goes the unspoken argument—the collusion.

This book is about being honest about a most unsettling problem: addictions. If the truth sets us free, as the Scriptures say, then deception keeps us enslaved to addictions. It's dishonest to say casinos bring in millions of dollars to state coffers without simultaneously talking about the ravages of gambling addictions. It's dishonest to talk about the joys of cooking and dining out without attending to our propensity to overeat. It's hypocritical to tempt consumers to spend more while burying our heads in the sand about credit card debt.

Half-truths are destructive. It's easy to say that gambling is just another form of entertainment, but there is a dark side as well. We obviously have to eat, and nothing is wrong with doing so—if our eating does not become excessive. Cell phones, television, and the Internet are just tools, and we're the ones who make them destructive. We're the ones lured by the temptations they offer, which results in the rationalization of our destructive behavior.

While not writing about addictions in particular, Dr. Harriet Lerner, in her book *The Dance of Deception,* discusses our strong tendency to pretend.

> Our failure to live authentically and to speak truly may have little to do with evil or exploitive intentions. Quite

the contrary, pretending more frequently reflects a wish, however misguided, to protect others and to ensure the viability of the self as well as our relationships. Pretending reflects deep prohibitions, real and imagined, against a more direct and forthright assertion of the self.[4]

Precisely.

We're not really setting out to deceive others so much as we want to be seen a certain way. We have good intentions. We also want to see others in a positive light. In the process, we participate, oftentimes unwittingly, in collusion.

Breaking the Silence

An obvious tension accompanies breaking the silence of collusion. You can't just walk up to a neighbor, husband, brother, or friend and say, "Hey, you're fat. You're going to kill yourself. Why don't you lose some weight?" Imagine if someone did that to you. I know that if someone waltzed uninvited into my life and began to preach to me about the dangers of caffeine, excessive work, or greed in my life, I'd first be dumbfounded and then annoyed. Finally, I'd want to give them a piece of my mind. I certainly wouldn't consider their advice to be rational and accurate—even if that were the case.

Most of us don't confront obvious problems with our mates and friends, let alone with complete strangers. Instead, we carefully guard our opinions and opt for silence when confronted with powerful issues and concerns. And that bothers me.

It's time to break the silence. Use common sense about when and where to confront others and when to share your own story. But break the silence. Transparency, as I discovered with Gregg, is refreshing and healing. We need to speak up if we are to reclaim our lives and our freedom. Addictions cause us to be riveted to the desire of choice, to focus our attention on it. This book is a cry for freedom, but achieving it will require some risk taking.

Perhaps breaking the silence means being honest with ourselves about our situation. Perhaps it means looking in the mirror and telling ourselves the truth. Later, we may decide to share this truth with others. First, however, we must be truthful with ourselves.

The psalmist says, "Search me, O God, and know my heart; test me and know my anxious thoughts. See if there is any offensive way in me, and lead me in the way everlasting" (Psalm 139:23).

Dedication to Reality

To pray for God to search us and know our hearts is the only path to authenticity and healing. But if an offensive way is in me, shouldn't I already know about it?

I still struggle with balance in my life. I've known the bondage of work addiction and acknowledged, in retrospect, the damage it did in my life. I've regretted lost years with my sons, unnecessary marital stress, and the toll on my health. I consider myself a recovering work addict, but that doesn't mean I can rest on my laurels. It means I must forever resist the inevitable temptation to add too much to my plate. Authenticity offers me an opportunity to know about my "slippery places" and take measures to guard against them.

Scott Peck insists that dedication to reality is a powerful tool for solving problems—and it is antithetical to collusion. In fact, he says that dedication to the truth is our path to healing and effective problem solving.

> The more clearly we see the reality of the world, the better equipped we are to deal with the world. The less clearly we see the reality of the world—the more our minds are befuddled by falsehood, misperceptions and illusions—the less able we will be to determine correct courses of action and make wise decisions.[5]

There is no surer way to lose perspective and direction than to deny, ignore, and collude with others about distant elephants. There is no surer path toward healing than to name the elephants, point out where they are, and comprise a plan to get them out of our lives. Recognition of and dedication to reality is the critical first step.

A Community of Sojourners

Repudiating collusion is not for the faint of heart. In fact, it can only be accomplished within a community of sojourners—like-minded folks who are willing to speak the truth. They're willing, like the psalmist, to pray, *Is there any offensive way in me? If so, lead me to freedom.*

There is comfort in knowing that others are on this journey as well, that we're all in this thing together. We're a parade of everyday addicts, but we can quit hiding and feeling shame about it. Facing these truths is the first and most powerful step toward healing.

Dan Allender, in his book *The Healing Path,* says, "A community of sojourners must leave the land of comfort and walk the healing path toward a better city than we enjoy now."[6] If we decide to join this band of truth tellers, we must be willing to say that the elephants are not off in the distance—they're right here in our midst, and they stink.

Allender says that author Gabriel Marcel defined community as the place where "I hope in you for us." Allender goes on to say, "The healing path is first and last about engagement. It is through engagement with you that I learn to hope more deeply for us. It is through hope that God slowly heals past brokenness on the basis of future promise."[7]

As we move through this book together, let's agree on these statements:

- We're all addicts.
- We can't deny it any longer.
- We won't support the mass collusion that creates the mass confusion.
- We need to name our addictions and begin the healing journey.

- The truth will set us free.

We're all in this together. Like Ken and Victoria, who struggle to name the elephants in their home and drive them out, we must courageously identify our own addictions and, with God's help, throw off their control. Like Ken and Victoria, who are finding their voice and courageously breaking their silence, we must be willing to initiate a conversation about this troubling topic. It all starts with us. We applaud Ken and Victoria and know they are gradually moving toward a healthier place. In the meantime, we've got to find our own healthier place.

As Marcel says, we're willing to hope for the best in others because we are connected to one another. Rather than winking at the dark places we visit, we're willing to hold hands and courageously name our addictions.

No more collusion. No more pretending. No more hanging on to the futile hope that the elephants will remain on the horizon. They're already here, in our homes and in our lives. Together we can drive them out.

CHAPTER THREE

DENIAL—Don't Even Notice I Am Lying

The worst lies are the lies we tell ourselves.
We live in denial of what we do, even what we think.
We do this because we're afraid.

RICHARD BACH

A LANKY YOUNG MAN with a friendly demeanor stopped by a local bar on his way home from a work. Along with his buddies, Jim joked about "working hard and playing harder." Stopping by this bar at night was as much a part of his routine as waking up and heading for his longshoreman's job each morning.

Every day after work Jim stopped by the Rusty Duck, where he ordered his usual—a Hefeweizen Pale Ale. The bartender knew him by name and had the beer pulled before he even sat down. Jim liked that. He felt comfortable at the Duck with his friends, his stool, and his drink. He even liked the smoky, dank smell. It was all very familiar, much like the bar in the long-running television show *Cheers,* where "everybody knows your name."

Jim also had a habit of smoking a joint in his truck on the way to the bar. Nothing heavy—"just enough to take the edge off a hard day at work."

But today something was different. When he plopped down on the bar stool next to his friends, they tried to engage him in conversation, but Jim wasn't his usual self.

"What's up with you, man?" one friend asked, looking at him quizzically.

"Just got some things going on," Jim said. "Nothing big. Everything's fine."

"If you say so," the man said, holding up his glass of beer with one hand and jabbing Jim in the ribs with the other. "Let's drink to the end of another day."

But things weren't fine. Jim knew it, and his friends could sense the difference. That evening he exchanged small talk with the others, but he skipped his traditional game of pool and couldn't muster anything close to his usual enthusiastic banter. Normally one to join in the laughter, tonight he struggled just to carry on a conversation.

The previous evening, Jim's wife of 15 years, Denise, had left him. She'd warned him repeatedly that if he kept going to the bar after work instead of coming home, she would have to consider leaving him. She told him that his marijuana use, along with the drinking, made an unbearable combination and that he needed to get some help. His only response was to tell her that his habits hurt no one.

Jim didn't think Denise was serious. He had always been able to muffle her critical voice. But this time, Denise wasn't buying.

"Enough is enough," she'd declared the previous evening. "I'm obviously not getting through to you. I'm not going to subject myself and the kids to this anymore. You continue to drink even after the doctor told you it was ruining your liver. And you say the marijuana doesn't affect you, but I notice a personality change. You're more irritable, you don't make goals or plans anymore, and you don't seem to be an emotional part of the family. You don't seem to care about my feelings or what this is doing to the kids. They're starting to ask questions, and I don't know how to tell them their father is a pothead and an alcoholic. I'm not going to put up with it anymore."

With that, she announced that she was taking the kids to her parents' house in a nearby town.

Jim had been drinking with "the boys" for more than ten years and had grown up with an alcoholic father. Several of the guys smoked marijuana and considered it part of their routine. These guys were, in a way, as much his family as his wife and kids. Being with them this evening took away some of the sting of her leaving.

Jim tried not to think about his wife and kids, but the beer wasn't strong enough to put them out of his mind. One part of him said it was time to straighten out his life and get the help she demanded he get. Another voice told him to have another beer and put aside his troubles for the evening. The latter approach had worked before, but he was less certain that it would work this time.

The Power of Denial

Jim watched his buddies play pool, laugh, and debrief about their day. But all he felt was numb. He couldn't stop thinking about his wife and kids leaving, but he found a special compartment in his brain to file the pain: the category called *denial*.

She'll be back once she realizes that she's making a mountain out of a molehill, he told himself. *She doesn't really want this situation for herself and the kids.*

He took deep gulps of beer, eagerly anticipating the rush he would feel when the alcohol hit his bloodstream. He had smoked some marijuana on his way to the bar, so he was already developing a good buzz.

You might be wondering how Jim can remain planted on his bar stool while his marriage is crumbling. How is it possible for him not to feel a thing, in spite of knowing that his life is completely out of control? The answer is simple—he's in denial.

Denial explains a lot of things when it comes to addictions because it helps people cope with their pain when they believe they have few other options.

And that's the key: Jim cannot face the fact that his life is out of control. That is the central element in denial—the need to believe that life is still manageable. He desperately wants to hold on to his world just as it is. He's grown to depend upon this bar, these friends, this beer. His world is constructed of these elements, and for years he's been able to have things his way. But not this time.

Let's consider the role of denial in Jim's life and imagine what he's been telling himself:

- *My drinking isn't hurting anyone.*
- *I work hard and deserve a few beers with my friends.*
- *My drinking doesn't stop me from being a good father.*
- *My wife will never really leave me.*
- *All my buddies are doing the same thing, and they're getting along just fine.*

These are but a few of the excuses Jim has used to "normalize" his drinking. His denial helps him believe that his life is manageable.

Denial keeps the pain at bay. It is a mechanism all of us employ to avoid agonizing thoughts and feelings. It offers a reprieve while we mull things over. Although Jim's wife and children can see the truth, Jim uses denial to pretend that everything is fine. Denial keeps the pain at a distance—at least for the moment.

Denial ultimately stems from underlying feelings of anxiety. This anxiety is rooted in deep fears that something bad is eventually going to happen, such as the loss of friends, family, or health. To some degree, pain is inevitable in our lives, so denial becomes our first line of defense against these uncomfortable feelings.

In Jim's case, he uses denial rather than face the ugly prospect that his wife and children might leave him or that something worse might happen to him. The closer he gets to those painful thoughts, the more denial he uses.

This is not to say that we intentionally dip into a bucket of denial, taking more and more as we need it. Quite the contrary—denial is primarily an unconscious process used to mitigate pain. In fact, it takes effort *not* to rely on denial. Facing reality demands effort and courage.

Denial in Small Doses

It's easy to criticize Jim while we tell ourselves that we're not in his boat. We're not drinking every day. We aren't smoking marijuana. We haven't put our spouse and our children off to the side. You may read Jim's story and assure yourself that you're not in his shoes, that your life is still manageable—but be careful. We all use denial every day in many different kinds of situations. You don't need to be a late-stage alcoholic or a daily user of drugs in order to fall victim to denial's power.

In some cases, denial is a good thing. It allows us to manage the ups and downs of life. Denial helps us cope with the dangers of war, the possibility of job layoffs, financial stresses, and even the challenges and dangers that face our children every day. Were we to face the immensity of our struggles all at once, we'd be overwhelmed.

But in many situations, denial is far more destructive than beneficial. Why? Because denial prohibits us from facing important truths.

Just the other day a woman called me to discuss her marriage. She indicated that her husband was a compulsive "saver" and that he controlled their finances like a watchdog. Although this problem may not sound severe to others, she said his miserly attitude created no end of bitterness in their marriage. Efforts to negotiate with him were fruitless. She couldn't buy needed clothes for her antiquated wardrobe, she felt inhibited from eating out with friends, and she had little idea as to their financial status. She called me for advice.

Here we see a man addicted to money—and in apparent denial about the destructive impact it was having on his marriage of 25 years. She, on the other hand, talked about trying to live with his habits, which merely enabled the problem to continue. Although she periodically vented her anger, she always relented, and they drifted back into relating in the same old ways, burdened by the same old problems.

I imagine that if I talked to him, he'd say, "We're doing fine. My method of managing our finances isn't hurting anyone."

Meanwhile, his wife told me, "I just live with things most of the time. I try to block his controlling behavior out of my mind."

Both are being dishonest. Their marriage is in trouble, and the longer they refuse to face the issue and work to resolve it, the worse things will get. How bad will things have to be before they acknowledge the severity of their problems?

Another Point of View

Dr. Lance Dodes, author of *The Heart of Addiction,* sees denial differently than many experts do. Rather than sticking with the traditional explanation that denial is used to avoid pain, Dodes writes, "At the heart of addiction is the necessity to defy helplessness." It's not the pain people are trying to deny as much as the feelings of helplessness they are experiencing.

Dodes, an addiction specialist and psychiatrist, doesn't see denial simply as a means to avoid reality. Because he believes the defense of denial is an effort to hang on to some level of control and power, Dodes says, "I have found that when people come to see that addiction is fundamentally an effort to retain power, rather than evidence of weakness or powerlessness, this alters the question for them."[1]

Dodes uses a unique method to break through the denial. Rather than asking people if they are addicts, he encourages alcoholics, drug users, and other addicts to retain some sense of empowerment over their lives. When this occurs, he finds that denial disappears. Rather than launching a direct assault on their denial, Dodes asks clients to consider the possibility that they can look at their situation in other ways. He invites them to view their lives from a larger perspective.

For example, rather than say, "Can't you see you're in denial?" he's more likely to say, "Is it possible that your drinking is causing more problems than you realize?" He's found this "softer" approach to be more effective than a traditional frontal assault because it allows people to maintain some sense of control over their lives, which Dodes feels is critically important. Individuals aren't pressed to defend their lifestyle; rather, they are invited to explore their life and choices.

Denial may allow us to feel in control of our lives, but if we're not truly in command, the denial only serves to feed our self-deception. The bottom line is that we need to face reality. We need to know if our liver is being rotted by booze; if our brain is being anesthetized by marijuana; if our physical, emotional, and spiritual lives are deteriorating under the influence of myriad temptations. We need to know that bitterness and resentment toward our mate are strong signals that something is wrong and that we need to address a problem.

Gradual Process

As you can probably imagine, Jim's life didn't suddenly spin out of control one Tuesday evening after work. It has been careening toward disaster for months, even years. Likewise, he didn't erect walls of denial in one fell swoop—he has taken years to learn to tune out the painful consequences of his behavior. Such is the case with any addiction.

As we learned in the last chapter, it often takes a family, city, and society to reinforce denial. While responsibility surely lies squarely on Jim's shoulders, we must take note of the social, familial, and generational issues at work. Jim's father was an alcoholic. He learned early on that "real men" stop by the tavern after a hard day at work. He also learned that longshoremen are a tough and hardy bunch, taking pride not only in how hard they work but also in how much liquor they can hold. They pride themselves on being gutsy, being fiercely independent, and listening to no one but their peers—most of whom are unlikely to confront addictive behavior.

Jim's wife, Denise, had threatened to leave before but never had the courage to follow through. She watched for years as Jim's drinking escalated, all the while making excuses for her husband's behavior. At first, she gently reminded him that his time at the tavern bothered her. She became increasingly irritated, but he responded to her irritation with excuses and rationalizations. He had a way of making it all sound so normal. Many times Jim said nothing when she got angry, which made arguing with him even more difficult.

Jim's behavior was so normal that his two children, a son and daughter, weren't clear why they were leaving to stay with their grandparents. Though they had a sense that something was wrong, Denise had largely protected them from the escalating problems. They hadn't seen many of their parents' squabbles, and most of the time their mother kept her frustration to herself. In many ways they were shielded from their father's slow-growing addiction.

But Denise has reached her boiling point. Uncertain as to what her next step will be, she knows she needs time and safety to think things through. Her parents' home offers a loving environment from which to contemplate her next step.

Stages of Denial

If we knew the trouble we could get into, that the light at the end of the tunnel was a fast-moving and deadly train, surely we'd be more careful with caffeine, nicotine, sexuality, food, gambling, shopping, and the like. Or would we?

At some level, we know that when we light that first cigarette, we're playing with fire. When venturing onto that pornographic website, we have at least a slight inclination that trouble is on the horizon. Even something as innocuous as shopping—spending money on credit—sends at least a dim alert. Denial begins during those early moments.

I won't be the one to get hooked, we insist. *I can stop any time I want.*

And so it goes. From the first moment we tiptoe into that forbidden (or sometimes not forbidden) territory, we run the risk of becoming ensnared. From the very beginning, we don't want to acknowledge that we might be headed for trouble. Gerald May highlights this:

> Not only does the person not recognize that a problem exists, she doesn't want to think about it. She doesn't see any reason to even consider it. This is denial. Evidence for addiction may be perfectly obvious to other people, but it is as if the addicted person is either completely blind to it or always looking in another direction.[2]

May goes on to note that denying the presence of the problem takes greater and greater energy. People may slip easily and painlessly into addiction to a substance or behavior, but they require more and more denial to avoid the problem.

Denial includes several stages:

Stage one denial. The person refuses to admit that a problem exists. In spite of overwhelming evidence to the contrary, the individual adamantly insists everything is fine.

Overcoming this level of denial is very difficult. If people have already determined that no problem exists, trying to coerce them into thinking differently is not likely to work. Very little, short of an intervention (to be discussed later in the book) or hitting bottom can shake them into seeing things differently.

Stage two denial. In this stage, people have admitted they have a problem but deny needing any kind of support. This is often called the pink-cloud syndrome. Addicts in recovery may revel in their newfound sobriety but see no need to take precautions against relapse.

I have met and worked with many people who are proud of themselves for facing their addiction. Having seen the light, they now believe themselves strong enough, smart enough, brave enough to avoid slipping back into the same old turmoil. They don't need crutches. Sadly, having failed to navigate this stage of denial, many relapse. In fact, studies show that those who fail to take recovery seriously are more vulnerable to relapse.

Stage three denial. Here, people may be willing to participate in a recovery program for a time but are unwilling to make a full commitment to "go to any length" (as prescribed by Alcoholics Anonymous and other recovery programs) to deal with the addiction.

Individuals in this stage of denial often have a narrow view of recovery. They wrongly believe that if they simply quit drinking or using or indulging in the addictive behavior for a time, they are working their program. They fail to realize that recovery is a never-ending process that demands physical, emotional, and spiritual regeneration.

In each stage of denial, pride can present a formidable obstacle. Even in the third stage, individuals frequently maintain a willfulness to do things their way. They refuse to submit to a higher power and to fully let go of their old and destructive ways of living.

Successfully moving through these stages requires complete submission. It takes an emotional acceptance that your life is out of control, accompanied by an ongoing spiritual submission to a recovery process that allows God to regenerate your broken heart and life.

I'm reminded of King Saul, who appeared addicted to power. He was initially reluctant to take the throne, but he was chosen to be the first king after a nation ruled by judges. A mighty warrior, he ruled decisively, though when given instructions by the Lord, King Saul was stubborn and rebellious. His addictive pride and greed prevented him from focusing on his duties of national security, moral leadership, and obedience to the Lord. Ultimately he spent endless hours and days in a paranoid hunt for his faithful army general, David, whom he considered a rival.

Although partially obedient, he often took matters into his own hands, doing things his own way. The prophet Samuel reprimanded Saul and told him he would no longer be king: "To obey is better than sacrifice, and to heed is better than the fat of rams. For rebellion is like the sin of divination, and arrogance like the evil of idolatry. Because you have rejected the word of the LORD, he has rejected you as king" (1 Samuel 15:22-23).

Saul had failed to learn a most essential lesson. Moving beyond addiction and into recovery means moving through each stage of denial and submitting our lives to an authority beyond and above ourselves. As the saying goes, "Our best thinking got us here." We might consider listening to others for a change as a means to get us out.

One Hundred Forms of Self-Deception

Jim's wife, Denise, still can't believe Jim is sitting on a bar stool at the Rusty Duck at a time when she's in a crisis. She's taken his children, whom she knows he loves, and walked out the door. She's incensed that he would rather hide in a bottle than tackle his addiction. Even in the face of this tragedy, Jim did little to try to convince her to stay. How can this be?

His behavior can be explained by denial. We can dissect the progression of denial and discover smaller ingredients to this process. These ingredients, all forms of self-deception, are called *thinking errors.* By exploring them, we'll learn more about our own addictive processes and the addictive processes of those we love.

Rationalization. Rationalization involves the thinking we use to explain away our behavior. We make something that is irrational, rational. Even while sitting in that smoky bar, Jim tells himself that what he's doing isn't really a big deal. He looks around and sees his friends doing the same thing and assures himself that his actions can't be *that* bad.

Consider how you use rationalization to make your irrational, immature behavior okay. What are the small sins in your life that you rationalize to silence the inner critic—your conscience?

Justification. Justification is much like rationalization. We justify our behavior, or define it as just and perhaps even righteous. This thinking error takes rationalization one step further—to the point of making our behavior seem right.

Jim can tell himself and his wife that he has a right to stop by the bar after work. After all, he works hard. He brings in the majority of the family income and is entitled to some respect. He works 50 and sometimes 60 hours a week, often volunteering for overtime. He lives on five and six hours of sleep. He gets dirty and tired. All so his wife and kids can have a nice home and a good life. These are his justifications for indulging in a little harmless drinking and drug use.

Minimization. Jim actually doesn't admit to drug use because in his mind, marijuana is not a drug like other "heavier" drugs. When his wife insists that marijuana *is* a drug, he won't concede. The only thing he is doing is smoking a little marijuana. Nothing major. Certainly nothing that would justify her noisemaking.

Procrastination. Many (if not most) addicts don't completely deny their problem. They have some sense that things aren't right. They're not oblivious to the growing distance in their marriage, the dollars foolishly spent, or the ravages of poor nutrition on their health. Many aspects of addictions simply cannot be ignored.

So with a nagging belief that things must change, they postpone their decision to get help. *Someday,* they reason. *I'll get to it someday.* Not surprisingly, someday never comes.

Stanton Peele, author of *7 Tools to Beat Addiction,* says, "Many wait for just the right time to change, when the costs of addiction are so great that change is unavoidable. We can imagine the perfect situation for kicking the addiction; we're just not there yet."[3]

Victimization. Playing the role of the victim is a particularly powerful form of denial. Not only is Jim, in his view, not doing anything wrong, he's actually the one being mistreated. After all, his wife and children have left him over something trivial. He's being victimized, and he feels entitled to being angry.

Playing the victim is a virile form of denial. Not long ago, during a couples' marriage session, a wife confronted her husband about his workaholicism. He shifted deftly into playing the victim. Without missing a beat he said, "I can't do anything right for you. You're always on my case. I work hard for the family, and you thank me by criticizing me. I'm the one who should be complaining."

His wife was speechless—and so was I. We were momentarily caught up in his victimization, by which the focus is turned against the criticizer.

One moment the wife was sure of her position, confronting her husband on his lack of emotional and spiritual availability. The next she was challenged for being an insensitive, unforgiving wife. Talk about a powerful tactic!

Blame. Playing the victim is a cousin to blaming. Blame, of course, involves criticizing and attacking others, finding fault for their behavior. I'm not talking about legitimate confrontation in marriage. I'm talking about situations in which people set up a smokescreen of blame in order to keep the focus off themselves.

"I'm not the one who needs to change," they say. "You do. You ought to look in the mirror before pointing fingers at me."

It might also sound like this: "Sure, I drink and smoke a little dope. But I wouldn't spend so much time at the tavern if things were more pleasant around the house. You're tough to live with."

Excuses. We can all find a thousand excuses for doing the things we do. There's always a reason for drinking, smoking, overeating, gambling, or whatever.

It sounds something like this. *I drink because all my buddies do it. I smoke because it helps me relax. I look at pornography because my wife doesn't give me enough sex. I shop because it makes me feel good. I sit for hours in front of the television because it takes my mind off things. I don't change because* (insert excuse here).

Distant elephants. Yes, we learned about this thinking error in the last chapter. We learned how we can become adept at thinking the problem is "out there" and that it will take years, perhaps a lifetime, to get "in here." The elephants are on the distant horizon, but they aren't stinking up our house yet.

Jim has mastered the art of denial, to his own demise. He's on the brink of losing his wife and children, and his denial is a shield against painful feelings. But it also walls him into a life without change and correction.

Perhaps you can relate. Consider your areas of weakness and addiction. How do you stop yourself from facing painful truths? How do those tactics protect you, and how do they insulate you from needed change?

Dead-End Thinking

Denial is particularly lethal because it locks our minds into thinking one particular way instead of embracing new possibilities and change. Denial creates black-and-white, rigid thinking. Denial says, *I'm this way, and I'm going to stay this way.* Conversely, freedom thinking says, *I've been this way, but with God's help and the support of others, I'm going to change.*

Denial is terribly frustrating to the spouse and family of the person in denial. Family members can recognize the addict's dead-end, destructive thinking. The people in denial see a light at the end of the tunnel, but their families know the light is a freight train.

This narrow thinking sullies any relationship, especially marriage. Relationships are built on the free flow of information. Vibrant marriages are built on each partner's freedom to share information. In a marriage rampant with thinking errors, communication becomes stilted, with certain conversations considered off limits. This approach severely restricts the growth of the relationship.

Jesus was familiar with those who had closed minds. He'd been preaching the truth, which was admittedly hard to hear. When His disciples asked why He spoke in parables, Jesus, in apparent frustration, said of the people, "Though seeing, they do not see; though hearing, they do not hear or understand...For this people's heart has become calloused; they hardly hear with their ears, and they have closed their eyes. Otherwise they might see with their eyes, hear with their ears, understand with their hearts and turn, and I would heal them" (Matthew 13:13,15).

The Irony of Denial

Denial includes a pathetic irony. We use it to find relief, but it leads us further into bondage. Every layer of denial we use at the start of our addictive process is a layer we'll have to carve away when we begin healing. The very activity or substance that we turn to for relief is actually part of the chain that keeps us in bondage and wreaks havoc in our lives.

Our friends, colleagues, and family members can often see the blind spots of our addictive behavior. Our spouse sees our dysfunctional eating habits as our weight increases and we put ourselves in physical jeopardy. But we offer excuses, alibis, and rationalizations. We don't want the truth.

Our mate sees us work ourselves into the ground "for the sake of the family," but we offer excuse after excuse to rationalize our workaholic behavior.

Our friends and family watch as we spend more and more time at the casino, rationalizing our behavior as leisure activity. They know better, but we refuse to hear them.

Others would like to help us with our secret sins, those that only we know about. But we choose to isolate ourselves, living disingenuously. We put up a front, shielding those who love us from knowing our darker habits. We know enough of the truth to hide our behavior from others. Our hearts become hardened as we strive to rationalize our behaviors. Soon, we can't discern the truth from the lies.

The irony of denial is that it numbs our pain at first, making us feel better in the short run, while killing our souls, spirits, and sometimes our bodies in the long run. We must endure the pain of withdrawal and face our inner demons in order to rid ourselves of our destructive habits.

Path to Freedom

Jesus offered the path out of denial and addictions and into freedom: "Blessed are your eyes because they see, and your ears because they hear" (Matthew 13:16). The gospel, or good news, is about hearing and receiving the truth. This is our path out of denial and into freedom—through hearing, accepting, and understanding the truth.

Alcoholics Anonymous proclaims that the path to sobriety is "rigorous honesty." Through much hard work and utilizing the 12 steps, alcoholics in recovery go through an arduous process of examining their lives. The fourth step is especially challenging: Individuals must participate in a "rigorous moral inventory," where they dissect their lives. Part of this includes identifying whom they've hurt and making amends when appropriate.

Those willing to dedicate themselves to the truth in this community of sharing, strength, and hope often find new freedom. However, newcomers are warned that if they truly want to throw off their addiction and their denial of it, they must be willing to go to whatever lengths necessary to remain sober.

Jesus uses similar language. Speaking in a parable, He said, "The kingdom of heaven is like treasure hidden in a field. When a man found it, he hid it again, and then in his joy went and sold all he had and bought that field" (Matthew 13:44).

Can you imagine wanting something so badly that you would give everything for it? Jesus says the kingdom of heaven is worth that price. Short of the kingdom of heaven, I can imagine nothing of greater value than freedom from addiction. But let us again consider what this requires of us:

- hearing the truth of our addictive behaviors
- receiving the fullness of this truth into our hearts
- emerging from our state of denial
- understanding this truth and applying it to our lives

Thus far, I've made the point that we're an addicted society. Even worse, our culture, society, and perhaps even our churches enable our addictions. Refusal to talk about these addictive behaviors reinforces them. We're a parade of addicts, and the extent that we admit that and talk about it is the extent to which we face the truth leading to freedom. Few are exempt from slipping into some form of addictive behavior, and fewer still are willing to face the full extent of their addiction.

In this chapter we've acquainted ourselves with the particulars of denial and how this process keeps us from healing. We discussed how denial is actually a form of deception—a process we use with ourselves as well as with others, to our own detriment.

Next we will turn our attention to specifics about addiction. For example, why does one person turn to drugs while another turns to television? Why does one become obese while another nearly dies from anorexia?

You've probably picked up this book because you recognize compulsive behaviors in yourself or someone you love. Remember, there is no shame in admitting powerlessness over an addiction. Recognizing that we can make healthy choices will move us along our path to freedom.

PART TWO

The Addiction *Lurking* in Your Home

Chapter Four

The Anatomy of Addictions

*Let us throw off everything that hinders
and the sin that so easily entangles, and let us
run with perseverance the race marked out for us.*

Hebrews 12:1

If there was ever a *Leave it to Beaver* family, it was mine. Born on the right side of town, the right side of the tracks, and even the right side of the street, I shouldn't have had a care in the world. My father was a sales manager for a wholesale sundry goods company. My mom was a stay-at-home mother until we five kids were in school, when she began a teaching career.

Our family had no drug or alcohol issues. No physical violence. No sexual trauma or generational poverty. Our life was based on old-fashioned, middle-class values and church three times a week. And yet despite all those advantages, I became an addict. When I look back on my childhood, I can find few predictors that would foreshadow my addiction to work. I wasn't a type A personality as a child. In fact, I was quite the opposite: type D-minus, as my high school grades indicate.

The only hint came in the form of a hard-driving father. What I lacked in ambition, he made up for in drive. I was the master of laziness and adolescent aimlessness, but he epitomized determination and focus.

I was also raised in a culture of hard work. The dominant industries in Bellingham, Washington, were logging, paper, and fishing, and men were proud of how hard they worked. Perhaps some of this ethic seeped into my veins without my awareness, though it certainly took time to take hold. I'm still not sure these are reasons for my eventual addictive behavior, but they are the only clues I've found.

My own case proves that there aren't always predispositions for our addictions and compulsions. Certainly, a history of violence or abuse can set the stage for adult problems. If you were raised in a family with generational alcohol abuse, you will be predisposed to those problems. If raised with parents who smoked marijuana in front of the kids, you learned too much, too early. But stereotypes don't provide consistent answers. Addictions can crop up anyplace and anytime.

I slipped out of high school on a wing and a prayer. The armed forces wouldn't take an asthmatic, and I didn't want to follow in my dad's footsteps. That left college. With the same lack of exuberance I exhibited in high school, I meandered through my first two years of college. I was biding my time, hoping some grand life direction would come and bite me on the backside. It didn't.

And then, very slowly, *it* began. I started getting an emotional high from earning good grades. Having struggled so much with academics in earlier years, I was certain I would flunk out of college. Initially, I thought college was the domain of rocket scientists, but with a dollop of encouragement from my professors, with a

C-plus here and a B-minus there, I began to wonder if I could do even better.

As I look back, I see hints of the addiction in those early college years. Desperate for life direction, I put more effort into earning good grades. Slowly but surely, I began to excel. I discovered the power of my gift of gab, my "charming personality," and my ability to communicate in writing. My grades skyrocketed. I went from C's to A's, and the rush of self-confidence was heady.

I graduated magna cum laude with a bachelor of arts degree and was on the dean's list several times. I received plenty of recognition and was proud of my accomplishments. It was big stuff for a boy who had always seen himself as an underachiever.

Having conquered the world of college, I wondered if I had a chance of doing the same at graduate school. It was more a lark than anything, or so I thought. My work addiction picked up steam. I excelled in graduate school, again achieving honors, and decided that if one graduate degree was good, two would be better. After obtaining my master's degree in social work, I went on to obtain master's and doctorate degrees in psychology. After that, I was red hot and rolling. My work engines were burning rocket fuel. I was determined, focused, rigid in my pursuits—common themes for those with addictive and compulsive behaviors.

With accolades pouring in from scholastic success, I went to work in a counseling practice and began experiencing financial freedom. I was not only becoming a workaholic but also accumulating compulsively—another addictive process. Bigger and better houses, cars, boats—anything I wanted, I purchased.

But what about my family? Having been married several years earlier, and with two young boys to raise, I was all but absent during their early years. My two young sons wondered where daddy was. My wife made it very clear that she was dissatisfied with my time away from home. She resented the late evening hours at work, but her complaints fell on deaf ears. I was out of control, focused entirely on work and material success.

My obsession with school and work lasted more than 20 years before I crashed. Sixty-hour workweeks finally took their toll. Almost overnight I was emotionally and physically exhausted. I could no longer sustain my energy and focus and was forced to cut back on work—ultimately a blessing in disguise.

Had it not been for a failing marriage and struggles with anxiety and stress, I might still be burning the candle at both ends. With the emotional unraveling, which often happens with addicts, I recalibrated my life. Due primarily to exhaustion, I cut back on work, reestablished my relationship with my wife, and renewed my relationship with my sons. Nothing, however, can bring back those lost years.

Expect No Respect

My story reinforces the notion that addictions have no respect for people. Having been insulated from drugs, alcohol, pornography, sexual abuse, and criminality throughout my childhood, I still became an addict. Practically raised in the church, with biblical and ethical principles coming out my ears, I still became obsessed with accomplishment, accumulation, and appearance.

Addictions and compulsions can strike anyone, anywhere. It doesn't matter whether you were raised in a wonderful family with the highest moral and ethical values, or whether alcohol and drug use have been rampant among your relatives for generations. Addictive and compulsive behaviors aren't about whether we are good people but rather about our character makeup and predispositions. We live in a society that reinforces addictions. Our weaknesses often come to the fore when we are tempted.

I am in no way casting blame or responsibility on anyone but myself, but society does reinforce certain addictions—work being one of them. Our society praises those who work harder and longer. Ironically, our society sees this addiction as being somehow healthy, but the results are anything but that.

Other societies, such as the Japanese, not only praise those who work long and hard but also expect their workers to do so. The Japanese even have a word for working yourself to death—*karoshi*, "death from overwork."

If you look around, you'll notice other addicts. You'll see the obvious signs of an addictive relationship to food, though you may not necessarily know about people's struggles with binging and purging or the use of laxatives. You know about your friend's habit of gambling at the casino, but you don't know how many times he's spent the family paycheck at the blackjack table. You sense that your friend's drinking is excessive, but you may not know the chaos created in the home as a result of his alcohol abuse.

We often see the early vestiges but are not always privy to the nuances and escalation that lead to addiction. Few people recognized that my life was spinning out of control. Few know that I still must guard against compulsive work tendencies or that I force myself to weave in vacations as a way to break up my obsession with work.

Anne Wilson Schaef, in her groundbreaking book *When Society Becomes an Addict,* says, "When work becomes an obsession, compulsive behaviors develop that can be harmful and even death-producing. As in accumulating money, gambling, sex, or any other process addiction, the act itself [working] loses its intrinsic meaning."[1] Such was certainly the case in my life.

Addictions and compulsive behaviors envelop us. We're swimming in a sea of addictions, and the first step out is to acknowledge our dependencies. We cannot change our chaos if we cannot name our chaos, and often those around us won't challenge us about our addictions, thus enabling us to continue spinning out of control.

How do things go from normal to excessive to abusive? How did my work drift from healthy and normal to a havoc-creating addiction? Let's explore the inner dynamics of addictions. Although they certainly aren't all the same, we can find many similarities. My guess is that you'll be able to connect your particular addiction or compulsion to the following explanations.

Biochemical Addiction

Addictions are sociological, psychological, biochemical, and spiritual phenomena. Just as surely as treatment must encompass each of these arenas, so too must our understanding of the growth of addictions.

Dr. Norman Doidge, in his fascinating book *The Brain That Changes Itself,* reminds us of the very definition of addiction: "All addicts show a loss of control of the activity, compulsively seek it out despite negative consequences, develop tolerance so that they need higher and higher levels of stimulation for satisfaction, and experience withdrawal if they can't consummate the addictive act."[2]

This is a well-accepted definition. Doidge, however, goes far beyond this description and helps us understand how addictions involve an unhealthy transformation of the brain: "All addiction involves long-term, sometimes lifelong, neuroplastic changes in the brain. For addicts, moderation is impossible, and they must avoid the substance or activity completely if they are to avoid addictive behaviors."

This is true with substance addictions to drugs, alcohol, or other substances, and it's also true with process addictions, such as to work, sex, or eating. As we learned earlier in the book, all addictions change our brain functioning.

Dr. Doidge reminds us that the neurotransmitter dopamine is at the root of most addictive and compulsive processes. Dopamine is called the reward transmitter because it is released in conjunction with certain drugs and activities. We obtain a surge of energy, pleasure, and even confidence.

Unfortunately, these repeated surges of dopamine play havoc with the plasticity of the brain. The same surge of dopamine that thrills us also changes our chemistry. We quite literally become different people in the way we think, feel, and behave. According to Dr. Doidge, the addict experiences cravings because his brain has become sensitized to the drug or the experience. Sensitization is different, however, from tolerance. As tolerance develops, the addict needs more and more of the substance or process to reach the desired level of pleasure. Sensitization leads to the need for less and less of the substance in order to crave it intensely.

Sexual Addiction

I commonly have two or three men addicted to pornography on my caseload. Just as surely as I've seen gambling addiction increase, sexual addiction seems to be on the rise as well.

Jake, a tall, thin man with a somber presence, came to see me after his wife kicked him out of the house. She'd repeatedly caught him viewing pornography on the Internet, but in spite of her threats he did not change his behavior. A 40-year-old professional, Jake was at a loss to explain his behavior.

Running his hands through his thick, graying hair and obviously distraught, Jake shared his circumstances.

"She checked my computer and found that I'd been watching porn again. Stupid of me because I knew she'd catch me. It's weird because I don't think I'm really hooked on that stuff, but sometimes I just can't stay away from it."

As we explored his history, he sounded much like some of the men Dr. Doidge discusses in his book, those who seek the stimulation of pornography but may actually not be gaining that much pleasure from it. Their behavior is compulsive—often done without thought or premeditation.

"Since neurons that fire together, wire together, these men got massive amounts of practice wiring these images into the pleasure center of the brain, with the rapt attention necessary for plastic change." Doidge goes on to explain that these men can conjure up these images and receive a shot of dopamine long after they are away from their computers.

Again and again, without fully realizing it, they can dial up images and get a dopamine surge. The same is true with other imaginings we create in our minds. Images and memories can bring us pleasure again and again, reinforcing the activity and reinforcing a change in our wiring.

I asked Jake whether he reviewed pornographic images throughout his day.

"Yes," he said soberly. "There are certain sites I like, with certain kinds of images. I look at them on the Net and then picture them again in my head. I started out slow as a teenager, but I'll admit my dependency on pornography has picked up speed as an adult. You'd think I'd give it up if I knew I was hurting my wife. I was afraid it might come to this. Now look at me. Out of the house, away from my kids, and feeling incredibly dirty."

"It's not that simple," I said. "And if I have a chance to talk with her, your wife may come to understand that it's not that simple. Once something becomes an addiction, we can't just turn it off. It's like a switch gets stuck, and we lose the ability to turn it off and on. Does that make sense?"

"Well, that's sure the way it was for me," Jake said. "But try explaining that to my wife. She's disgusted with me."

"She has a right to be upset, Jake," I said. "But I think that with some counseling she can come to realize that you weren't out to intentionally hurt her. You've been getting high off pornography for a long time, and your brain keeps seeking those highs. We've got to shift gears and talk about recovery."

"I'm ready," Jake said, tears running down his face. "I'm tired of feeling controlled by this stuff. I sure hope you can help."

"I can," I said. "But there's going to be some pain. Your brain is accustomed to its daily dose of pornography. Don't be surprised if you miss those moments of pleasure. Your brain has become accustomed to them even though right now you're reeling from the pain of it all."

Seeking Pleasure

Addictions and compulsive behaviors are rooted in the pursuit of pleasure, but this pursuit has always had its dark side. If a little bit of chocolate is good, a huge turtle pie slathered with fudge must be even better.

Dr. Archibald Hart, in his book *Thrilled to Death,* says, "While it is essential that the brain's pleasure system is kept in tip-top condition, we literally walk a tightrope here. Stay on the rope, and you will travel toward a rich and fulfilling life. Miss your step by pursuing pleasure too eagerly and greedily, and you can fall into the depths of despair."[3]

Hart goes on to say, "The greatest menace associated with greedy pleasure is that it can become a hidden addiction." He goes so far as to say that everything that gives us pleasure has the potential of becoming addicting. He lists the parade of addictions that have already been cited in this book. Many activities we take for granted can be abused. Television, sports, food, sex, bidding on eBay, and so on.

Dr. Hart explain what goes awry for the addict: "Behind all the factors that can create hidden addictions lies the overuse of our pleasure system through what I call *pleasure boosters*—extraordinarily stimulating activities that amplify the strength of the pleasure experience."[4]

These pleasure boosters are what I've referred to as hits or highs—memories from pictures on the Internet, from winning a large pot at the poker table, from binging at the door of the refrigerator, from working on an exciting project and receiving accolades, from betting on or watching the latest football game on the big screen, from using laxatives and feeling the loss of weight, from the stimulation of drugs or alcohol rushing to the brain.

With addictions, we get the thrill during the activity and during our remembering of the activity. When down, we can go to a file in our brain and bring up a pleasure boost. This action, if repeated, leads to addiction.

Avoidance of Creativity

Julia Cameron, author of *The Artist's Way,* believes that addictions also create havoc with creativity. In fact, she wonders if many use or abuse certain activities as a way to avoid their creativity. For many, the creative world is unknown and even uncomfortable.

> For some people alcohol is the favored block. For others, drugs. For many, work is the block of choice. Busy, busy, busy, they grab for tasks to numb themselves with…For others, an obsession with a painful love places creative choice outside their hands. Reaching for the painful thought, they become instant victims rather than feel their own considerable power.[5]

Cameron goes on to suggest that food, sex, work, and other activities are all good in themselves, but the abuse of them causes problems. Knowing yourself as an artist, she says, means acknowledging which behaviors or substances you abuse when you want to block yourself. You stifle your creative energy through a process of self-sabotage. Sometimes our potential frightens us, and we must find some way to slow ourselves down. What better way than to go back to our drug or activity of choice?

Actually, Cameron's observations aren't much different from Dr. Hart's or Dr. Doidge's. The artist feels a bit of frustration, and then, rather than dealing with the tension effectively, decides to escape instead. Frustrated that the words won't flow onto the page or that the colors won't move onto the canvas in the desired way, the artist reaches for the favorite "drug" to calm the inner tension rather than working through it. Of course, this doesn't solve anything but only makes things worse.

Escape from Tension

Seeking pleasure or avoiding pain? They are just two different sides of the same coin. Addictions are rampant, in part because we have such an intolerance for tension. We want to avoid suffering. We look for shortcuts. Finding them, we're tempted to return to them again and again, thereby sensitizing the brain to these hits.

If you have a headache, grab an aspirin. If you're anxious, reach for a tranquilizer. If discouraged, try an antidepressant. The problem that can develop from these solutions is that the deeper issue is never resolved, and we develop a habit of reaching for something rather than changing our attitude or circumstances.

Addictions are often a means of escape. Unwilling to look inside to see what might be bugging us, we want an immediate remedy, a quick fix, an instant solution.

One alcoholic man I knew said to me, "After a while, I found any reason to drink. If I was upset, grab a beer. If I was happy, grab a beer. If I had a fight with my wife, grab two beers. If I had a tough day at work, grab three beers. Any challenge or struggle was reason enough to drink. The problem was, I learned that I could never face anything without beer."

A repeated behavior becomes a habit. A repeated habit sensitizes the brain and creates "drug-experience seeking behavior." What starts out innocently enough turns into something that controls our lives.

Cycles of Behavior

So much about addictive and compulsive behaviors can be explained by repetitive actions. Feeling tension, we seek relief from the pain. Finding pleasure, we repeat the behavior again and again and again. We've learned that these repetitive actions literally create changes in brain chemistry, causing us to habitually repeat the performance. We receive emotional and biochemical hits that reinforce the habit patterns.

Dr. Patrick Carnes' seminal work on sexual addictions, *Out of the Shadows,* describes the cycles of sexual addiction. These patterned ways of behaving are apropos to other addictions and compulsive behaviors as well. In fact, I suspect they are present in all addictions.

Dr. Carnes says each addictive experience progresses through a four-step cycle that intensifies with each repetition:

1. *Preoccupation.* This is a trance or mood wherein the addict's mind is engrossed with thoughts of the behavior. This mental state creates an obsessive search for sexual stimulation.

2. *Ritualization.* The addict develops routines that lead up to the sexual acting out. The ritual, repeated over and over again, intensifies the preoccupation, adding arousal and excitement.

3. *Compulsive sexual behavior.* The addict engages in his favored sexual act, which is the end goal of the preoccupation and ritualization. Carnes says addicts cannot control or stop this behavior.

4. *Despair.* The addict feels utter hopelessness about his behavior.

This destructive cycle becomes self-reinforcing, as Carnes explains: "The pain the addicts feel at the end of the cycle can be numbed or obscured by sexual preoccupation which re-engages the addiction cycle."[6]

A review of these stages and this process suggests similarities between sexual addiction and other addictions. Again, while Carnes indicates that these stages fit the sexual addict, I see significant similarities with most other addictions.

I can easily apply these stages to my work life. Looking back, I see how I became preoccupied with work, success, and the accumulation of money and possessions. I gloated about how many hours I could work. I prided myself on being able to keep up with others who worked very hard.

I can also see how my behavior became ritualized. I did the same things day after day, gaining a high when I accomplished my work goals. I can also see how my work became excessive and led to episodes of despair because I knew I was out of control and hurting myself and my family. Then I'd start the cycle over again, ultimately leading to emotional exhaustion.

Degeneration

Sadly, the path of addictions is one-directional—downward to despair. There is no such thing as dabbling with addictive substances and processes, especially if you have a predisposition toward them. We've learned that the only choice one can truly make is recovery, leading to abstinence.

However, in the meantime, addictions create absolute havoc. They tear apart our families, destroy our emotional well-being, and annihilate our spiritual vitality.

I am always saddened when viewing the time-lapse images of someone addicted to methamphetamine. Let's say the first picture is of a beautiful blonde-haired woman with a bright smile, a clear gaze, and a lively disposition. Slowly, almost imperceptibly in the first few frames, she changes. She loses her smile and ever so gradually develops wrinkles in her brow and pockmarks on her face. In the latter frames, her teeth are decayed, her eyes sunken and hollow, and she appears to be gripped by sadness. The final picture is pathetic—she is lost. Jaundiced and vacant, her eyes search for hope. Gaunt and ugly, unkempt and disheveled, she has literally lost much of herself and her life.

But this doesn't happen with other addictions, does it? Well, yes and no. The physical degeneration may not be as severe, but the emotional, relational, and spiritual desolation is just as deep. Ask Jake, who risked losing his wife, home, and family. He is desperate for help in stopping the downward spiral.

Ask the man who just lost another $300 at the slot machines, money he needed to pay his monthly bills. Ask if his wife and family have been affected by his addiction.

Ask me about the lost years when my sons were young and rambunctious and needed a father. Ask me to describe now, in hindsight, how I was satisfied just to be around for the last ten minutes of their day. I'd give anything to have those days back. But they're gone, and I must live with the loss, the sadness, and the guilt.

Chasing the pleasures, avoiding the pain, we've all lost a lot. We've gotten hooked by cycles of reinforcing behavior that destroys us. Such is the nature of addiction.

Lusts of the Flesh

Dr. Carnes' language seems to echo a particular passage of Scripture in which the apostle James says, "Each one is tempted when, by his own evil desire, he is dragged away and enticed. Then, after desire has conceived, it gives birth to sin; and sin, when it is full-grown, gives birth to death" (James 1:14-15). It all begins with temptation. Who of us cannot relate to having some temptation that brings us immediate pleasure? Not willing to delay gratification, we want to ease the tension and gain relief and pleasure.

And where does this temptation come from? Our own desires. For some, it's chocolate. For others, exercise, the lottery, or the chat room. The Scriptures indicate that we must acquaint ourselves with our desires, for that's where the battle must first be waged.

Disordered desires lead to sinful behavior. Few of us stop at just the thought of something—we just do it. And when we do it again and again, we develop an addiction and compulsion. Now the behavior is larger than we are. Our little habit has gained momentum and become a monster that controls our lives.

The apostle James accurately describes what most of us have experienced: We're dragged away and enticed again and again. We no longer have complete choice. The enticement is greater than our power to resist.

And then, when our behavior is full-grown, it can lead to emotional, relational, and spiritual death.

Regeneration

Thankfully, our story doesn't end here. Throughout the remainder of this book we'll explore how we can gain victory over these desires, compulsions, and addictions. Jesus came to break our yoke of bondage to anything—including these addictions. He understands our powerlessness to them and offers hope.

James' message cautions us about our desires and reminds us that our desires often become excessive, leading to bondage. Having desires is normal, but they often become excessive and thus damaging to us. We lose focus, and our goals become askew as we seek to serve our addiction. We lose ourselves and our freedom in the process.

Jesus offers hope, healing, and regeneration. The apostle Paul is a study in regeneration. Paul was formerly Saul, a man addicted to power and to abusing Christians. He was a horrific man, rigid in his thinking and singular in his pursuit of killing Christians. He was most certainly a man in bondage.

But in the midst of "breathing out murderous threats against the Lord's disciples," he fell to the ground on the road to Damascus. In the days that followed, Saul would be transformed by the power of the Holy Spirit. No longer the murderer Saul, he became Paul, the follower of Jesus.

This kind of transformation is indeed miraculous. Ours might not be so dramatic, but we can be transformed as well. Through the regenerating power of the Holy Spirit we can be freed from the chains of addiction and compulsion. Our minds can be renewed, our emotions can be rebalanced, and much of what we have lost can be restored.

Jesus applied these words from the prophet Isaiah to Himself: "The Spirit of the Sovereign LORD is on me, because the LORD has anointed me to preach good news to the poor. He has sent me to bind up the brokenhearted, to proclaim freedom for the captives and release from darkness for the prisoners...They will rebuild the ancient ruins and restore the places long devastated" (Isaiah 61:1-2,4).

Jesus offers this kind of transforming, regenerating power to us. We'll learn more about specific addictions and the path of freedom from them as we move together through this book.

Chapter Five

Under the Influence

In my judgment, such of us who have never fallen victims [to alcoholism] have been spared more by the absence of appetite than from any mental or moral superiority over those who have. Indeed, I believe if we take habitual drunkards as a class, their heads and their hearts will bear an advantageous comparison with those of any other class.

Abraham Lincoln

WE'VE REVIEWED OUR PARADE of addictions, realizing that we, like so many others, are perhaps only a step or two away from falling victim to them. We've also explored how society reinforces our addictions. As Anne Wilson Schaef says in her book *When Society Becomes an Addict,* we're living in a culture that encourages and enables addicts.

Even if you're not currently struggling with an addiction, chances are you have such issues in your family history, and your life probably has been directly affected as a result. Maybe you've had a mother with severe codependence, a father with a sexual addiction, or a brother with a drug addiction. It's easy to understand why we all have everyday addictions.

We've learned about the anatomy of addictions—how we come to be addicts. Now it's time to zero in on some of the more prominent addictions. I want you to learn about the different aspects of addictions and how similar they are.

I've described how I have been impacted by my work addiction, but I'd also like to share the hidden alcoholism in my family background and the ripple effect it's had on me.

My paternal grandfather, Henry Hawkins Sr., died before I was born because of complications of alcoholism. I never really thought his life affected mine, but the more I learn about generational addictions, the more I see his hand on my life.

Letting go of denial is difficult—I don't want to acknowledge problems in my grandfather's life. Yet as I learn about the anatomy of addictions, I believe my grandfather's addiction cast a long shadow over my father's life and then my own. Perhaps your story has similarities.

As my father tells it—and he resists telling this story—his father began drinking heavily after World War I, and his life became consumed by the bottle. My grandmother struggled with multiple sclerosis, and after my grandfather's death, my dad and his younger brother, Larry, were forced to work.

My father's and uncle's lives were altered by their father's addiction. In their late adolescence their life became overly serious, at a time when life should have been more carefree. Responsibility became increasingly important.

My father clearly was affected by alcoholism. The shame of having an alcoholic father was large in that day—perhaps larger then than it is now. The father in the family was expected to be responsible, to care for his family, to hold down a job. My grandfather did few of those things.

"We did what we had to do," my father says matter-of-factly. "I knew how to work, and I did it."

My father developed an absolute intolerance for alcohol and those who used it, a radical swing often found in children of addicts. In fact, I've never seen my father or mother take a drink in their lives. They've made their disgust for alcohol known.

"Alcohol does nothing for anyone," my father once said. "It ruins lives. Why would I touch it?"

His argument is sound. He watched his father ruin his life and create undue stress on his own. At an early age, my father had to care for his ailing mother. At a time when my father should have felt carefree and alive with possibilities, he could think of only one thing—providing for his younger brother and his mother.

Where his father was irresponsible, my father was responsible. Where his father was addicted and obsessed with drink, my father was focused on taking care of his family. Where his father was tolerant of alcohol, my father was intolerant of it.

Children often become much like their parents, or in reaction to a negative situation, they become the opposite. This was the case for my father. He would have nothing to do with alcohol. He was self-controlled, perhaps to a fault. He was stern, disciplined, directed—all traits missing in his alcoholic father.

When I was able to fully comprehend his story, the pieces started to fall into place for me. After all these years, I simply thought my grandfather was an absent figure, one who had no influence on me. But that isn't true. His alcoholism affected me in ways I may never fully understand.

Today, I can sense the shame my father feels. I've seen it reflected in his silence. He has built walls between himself and the pain he felt from his father's alcoholism. He quieted the inner demons by working very hard. He provided for his five children and wife and did so in a way that would make any son proud. But his work became an addiction, reinforced and repeated over and over again.

His attitude toward work certainly influenced me. Not that he made me a work addict. I had many, many opportunities to ask for help but failed to do so. My father created a life around responsibility and work—play came after those other tasks were completed. I'm wired much the same way. Work comes first, play second. Play was something one could enjoy only after the work was done.

After a shaky start, I adopted those values wholesale, leading to my own work addiction.

Ripple Effect

As I've said, addictions cast a long shadow. We're learning that they influence each of our lives in some way. None of us have been spared the impact of addictive and compulsive behaviors. They affect us in ways we can explore and discover and in ways we will never fully understand.

My parents' disdain for alcohol was cast firmly into my ethical framework. Like most of the people in my family's social circle, we maintained an unspoken contempt for those who succumbed to alcohol abuse.

My father's prohibition against alcohol wasn't enough to stop me from dabbling with this powerful potion during high school and college, but it was enough to keep me anxious when I got too close to a predetermined edge. Being out of control has never been comfortable for me.

My grandfather's alcoholism affected his son as well as my generation. My siblings and I have never talked openly about our genetic predisposition to the problem, but the ripple effect is unmistakable.

The Neighborhood

By adolescence, I became aware of the hidden problems alcohol was causing among the families in our neighborhood. I was shocked to learn that two of my best friends' parents were alcoholics, though they were never called that at the time. Today, these friends tell stories of finding their parents passed out after the evening meal. During adolescence I also began learning about the hardworking, hard-drinking loggers and fishermen of our community. It was customary, even expected, that these men would go to the tavern after working in the woods or on the boat and drink a pitcher or two. I joined this fraternity as soon as I was old enough, and it became part of my lifestyle. I worked on the fishing boats and in the woods throughout college, and alcohol became a standard part of my weekend.

My parents were understandably disappointed. They watched with discouragement as I drifted into a world where I betrayed my family values.

Two disparate worlds—the abstinent and highly religious world and the hardworking, hard-drinking world—were separate but related in my early life. Some of the men with whom I logged, fished, and drank attended church with me. While clearly incongruous, somehow it all fit together.

Yet I was able to know "when to say when." This is surprising given my genetic history of alcoholism and compulsive behavior. Perhaps more than anything, I was lucky.

James Milam and Katherine Ketcham, authors of *Under the Influence,* state, "The weight of evidence clearly links alcoholism to heredity." They go on to say that children of alcoholics are much more likely to become alcoholics themselves—four times more likely.[1] My father could easily have become an alcoholic, but he made decisions early in his life to avoid people, places, and situations that would lead to such a problem.

My childhood buddies haven't been as fortunate. My friends, the children of alcoholics, have struggled with drug and alcohol abuse and addiction throughout their lives. In one of the families, alcoholism has been a debilitating factor for generations.

Alcohol-Related Statistics

Although I never recognized the devastating impact of alcohol on my friends or their parents, I can look back now and see it. My neighborhood was perhaps more normal than I knew.

According to the National Center for Health Statistics, America loves its alcohol. Consider these facts from 2006:

- Sixty-one percent of adults drank alcohol.
- Thirty-two percent of drinkers had five or more drinks on at least one occasion.
- There were 21,081 alcohol-induced deaths, excluding accidents and homicides.
- There were 12,548 alcohol-related deaths due to liver disease.

In spite of its harmful effects, alcohol plays a strong and central role in our culture. Alcohol is part of our youth and adult culture, and it's even a staple in our retirement culture.

Many people have their first experience with alcohol at an early age, with alcohol and drug use occurring at earlier and earlier ages. Most statistics suggest that the earlier people drink, the more likely they are to develop a clinically defined alcohol disorder at some time in their lives.

"The National Institute on Alcohol Abuse and Alcoholism now has hard evidence to support what many prevention specialists and parents have long assumed: Youthful experimentation with alcohol is not a benign rite of passage. It is a risk-filled practice that can have disastrous results."[2]

We might smile when recalling our youthful drinking days, but some of us may recognize the beginnings of a life replete with alcohol abuse. Some remember escapades involving drinking and driving, DUIs, and fatal crashes. Others recall risky sexual behavior, unwanted pregnancies, and abortions. They look back on foolish behavior and victimization of others. Drinking is not as innocent a behavior as we'd like to believe.

Prohibition

We have always had contradictory societal attitudes and

policies regarding alcohol. On one hand we've had an intolerance for alcohol abuse, but on the other we have a bar on every corner in most cities in America. We've created stricter laws about drunk driving and penalties for accidents caused by alcohol, and yet we celebrate drinking on television sitcoms, in advertisements, and as an integral part of Americana.

Years ago, we had a harsher attitude about alcohol, one that led to the National Prohibition Act of 1920. It abolished the manufacture, sale, and consumption of any alcoholic beverage with more than .05 percent alcohol. Prohibition was undertaken to reduce crime and corruption, solve social problems, and reduce the tax burden created by prisons. Although alcohol consumption reportedly declined for a few years, bootlegging became organized, and people obtained alcohol through indirect and criminal means. Many also began abusing other drugs, such as heroin, cocaine, and marijuana. Prohibition was considered a social failure, and the act was repealed in 1933.

The failure of the Prohibition Act proved that government cannot fully legislate abstinence from alcohol. It also demonstrated that personal responsibility is necessary and that alcohol addiction is a social, biological, emotional, and spiritual problem that cannot be remedied by the implementation of a single law.

To Imbibe or Refrain

The available information about alcoholism is confusing and at times seemingly contradictory. Alcoholism has been found to correlate to a number of factors:

- a family member who suffers from alcoholism
- a history of substance abuse
- a history of depression
- post-traumatic stress disorder
- peer pressure

- stress

- easy accessibility to alcohol

Everyone can choose whether or not to drink, but those with some or all of the above risk factors find themselves in greater jeopardy.

Still, the water is murky regarding who will and who will not become addicted. Who will be able to drink responsibly? Who will succumb to "problem drinking"? And who will develop alcoholism? We simply don't know why some people develop problem drinking, which creates occasional issues, while others move headlong into alcoholism, which affects every facet of their lives.

Dr. Donald Goodwin has written extensively about problem drinking and alcoholism. In his research he found that problem drinking appeared to be caused by psychological, emotional, or social problems, while alcoholism was more closely connected to hereditary factors. Goodwin's studies provide compelling evidence that most alcoholics do not drink addictively because they are depressed, lonely, immature, or dissatisfied. They drink addictively because they have a hereditary predisposition to alcoholism.[3]

This argument seems to be generally true, though not always. I, for example, have the genetic background of alcoholism, yet I have always been able to take it or leave it. While others seemed to be easily hooked by alcohol, I was able to dabble with it and retain choice about how much to drink. Again, this is surprising given my genetic makeup, but it is perhaps understandable given my parents' position on alcohol in conjunction with strong religious sanctions against it.

Although there is no ironclad cause-effect relationship in place for alcoholism, we do find predisposing factors. We know we must grapple with this notion of choice. As I've stated, we may choose to take the first drink but be burdened with so many risk factors that our ability to choose is severely compromised after that initial drink. If, for example, we have alcoholic parents, alcoholic grandparents, and other social and emotional problems, our ability to choose is severely weakened. At some point in the addictive progression, our ability to choose is all but absent.

I must emphasize again that we always retain the element of choice in our life path. Regardless of where you are in an addictive process, you can always choose to reach out for support and assistance in recovery, which we will talk about in depth later in this book.

A Disease or Not

I recently counseled a woman who had been referred by the courts for a mental health evaluation. It was a testy encounter.

Alice was 45 years old but appeared much older. She wore stained, loose-fitting jeans and a baggy sweatshirt, and she was at least 20 pounds underweight. She appeared uneasy, with an unsteady gaze and fidgety mannerisms.

"Could you tell me why you've been asked to undergo a mental health evaluation?" I asked.

"Got into a fight with my boyfriend, and we were both drinking," she said, shifting in her chair.

"Were you charged with anything?"

"That's still got to be decided," she said. "I have to do a drug and alcohol evaluation and this evaluation with you."

"Do you think you have a drinking problem?" I asked, glancing down at the police report she'd handed me when she arrived.

"I wouldn't call it a problem," she said. "I'm in treatment again, and they say I've got a disease."

"You've already started treatment?"

"Yep," she said. "I know they're going to make me go, so my attorney said to get a jump on things and get into treatment."

"And they say you've got a disease?"

"Like I said, it's not my fault. My parents were both alcoholics, so I didn't stand a chance. Both my sisters are alcoholics too. Runs in the family."

"Have you been in treatment before?"

"I went one or two times before, but it never stuck," she said. "I guess I just didn't take it seriously. This time I'm going to finish the program."

"Why didn't you finish the program previously?"

"You don't get it, do you?" she said. "I can't help it."

"Have you ever really given treatment a chance?"

"Maybe," she said. "I don't remember."

"Did you go to follow-up meetings after you went to treatment?"

"Nope. I don't think I finished any program."

Alice became increasingly irritated with me and my questions. She seemed impatient with the evaluation and repeatedly minimized personal responsibility for her problems. I'd heard the argument before—that an addict can't take personal responsibility because an addiction is a disease. The debate has raged for years and continues to this day. It is one of the most difficult controversies in the field of drug and alcohol addiction.

On one side are those who believe alcoholism is a disease. They say addiction or alcoholism is *not* a moral weakness but rather the result of a powerful chain of molecular events that lead a person to drink repeatedly. They insist it all has to do with the brain seeking another shot of dopamine, with some drinking binges offering ten times the normal amount in the brain. They point out that the pleasure doesn't last long, creating an increase in alcohol-seeking behavior. With some addictions, they argue, the brain chemistry actually changes, especially the nerve endings receiving dopamine.

Those on the other side of the debate say alcoholism or addiction is *not* a disease over which people have no control. They believe treatment can be quite effective in diminishing cravings. They say addicts' or alcoholics' brains are not always in a state of siege and insist that addicts take responsibility for their behavior and change their lives.

How powerless are alcoholics? Certainly people lose some of their ability to choose when they cross the line from social drinker to alcoholic. But has all choice been lost? I don't think so, and I don't think we would be wise to think of addiction from this perspective. Many believe, as do I, that what fuels the addiction epidemic is the belief that we are powerless in the face of temptation—which certainly runs counter to the Scriptures: "No temptation has seized you except what is common to man. And God is faithful; he will not let you be tempted beyond what you can bear. But when you are tempted, he will also provide a way out so that you can stand up under it" (1 Corinthians 10:13).

This is not to trivialize the power of an addiction or the impaired thinking that results from addiction. We are responsible to understand our family history and respond accordingly. If caught in the throes of addiction, we must take effective action. We can always choose to renew our minds through treatment. We can always seek help.

Another Bud

Just as surely as alcohol destroys the soul and spirit of an individual, family, and perhaps even community, another "Bud" is equally destructive. It's the marijuana bud. Although we could discuss countless illicit drugs in this book, I've chosen to focus on marijuana and methamphetamine because they are the most commonly abused illicit drugs in the United States.

Marijuana is a greenish brown mix of flowers, stems, seeds, and leaves of the hemp plant *cannabis sativa,* usually smoked as a cigarette or in a pipe. It has also been mixed in food or even brewed as a tea. It is called hashish in a more concentrated form. The main chemical ingredient in marijuana is THC (delta-9-tetrahydrocannabinol).

Marijuana is one of the most highly addictive illicit substances, although many users disagree. They tell themselves that marijuana is just an herb, but they fail to acknowledge its highly addictive properties or admit that marijuana has been repeatedly shown to be a "gateway" drug leading to other addictive substances. Nicotine is the most addictive substance, with about one-third of people who smoke becoming addicted. Nine percent of those who have used marijuana become addicted, according to the National Institute of Medicine.

I recently worked with a teenager, Brent, who used marijuana "recreationally." Once an honor roll student, Brent's grades had plummeted in recent months, coinciding with his increased marijuana use. Normally a likeable teenager, he'd become increasingly sullen and irritable. His parents sought my opinion regarding the increased problems with their son.

Brent's parents had caught him smoking pot repeatedly and resorted to periodic urinalysis to stop his habit. Even with the threat of these tests, Brent reluctantly admitted that he still smoked marijuana occasionally with his friends. He continued to use, all the while proclaiming that he could take it or leave it anytime he wanted.

In a family counseling session, Brent's father had put him to the test.

"Fine," his father told him, "then leave it!"

"You're making a big deal out of nothing," Brent retorted. "All my friends smoke pot, and they're getting along just fine."

That actually was not the case. His friends were using marijuana and were doing worse academically than their peers, had engaged in minor criminal acts, and were experiencing increased family problems.

This largely went unnoticed by Brent. In spite of his plummeting grades, increased tensions at home, and irritable disposition, he said his life was going well. Outward appearances to the contrary, Brent believed his life was fine. But his tired, unkempt appearance belied deeper problems. He vowed that his grades were not affected by his marijuana use and that they were on the rise. This did not seem to be true.

Such is the case with addictions—we may be the last ones to

notice our own downward spiral. Others may notice the physical and emotional deterioration while we deny the objective evidence. We often tenaciously cling to the belief that life hasn't changed.

Statistics reveal the severity of the marijuana problem among youth in the United States:

- In 2004, 14.6 million Americans age 12 and older used marijuana at least once in the month prior to being surveyed.
- About 6000 people a day in 2004 used marijuana for the first time—2.1 million Americans.
- Of these, 63.8 percent were under the age of 18.[4]

Like Brent, many of these kids say, "What's the big deal?" This is actually a common refrain of all addicts, but it's especially pronounced with marijuana users.

"But it's harmless," Brent insisted.

The research suggests the opposite, indicating that marijuana is mind-altering, creates addiction, is a gateway drug to "harder drugs," leads to lung cancer, and slows the smoker's ability to focus. Many chronic users experience "amotivational syndrome," a decrease in the user's drive and ambition.

Brent is a typical adolescent. He wants to be accepted by his peers, and many of his peers are smoking cigarettes and pot. They see marijuana use as harmless. They complain about uptight parents who complain about pot-smoking teenagers.

Having counseled dozens of kids like Brent and having worked as the psychologist on a drug and alcohol inpatient program, I've never believed marijuana was harmless. Can some people use it "recreationally" without becoming addicted? Yes, just as many people are able to drink alcohol without becoming addicted. But let's not lose track of the bottom line: Marijuana is an addictive, mind-altering substance with chronic and serious biological, social, psychological, and spiritual ramifications.

Meth

You won't see any cute halftime ads for methamphetamine. You won't see friends on a sitcom sitting at a club, laughing and joking about their day as they inject or snort a line of meth. You're not likely to hook up with pals at a social event and be invited to use meth with them.

Methamphetamine abuse is a brutal, debilitating addiction. It kills the soul, the psyche, and the spirit of its victims. We've yet to fully appreciate the chaos it creates in households across our country.

As with many other addictive substances and processes, meth does its damage by releasing very high levels of the feel-good neurotransmitter dopamine into the system. Methamphetamine use is quickly addicting, and chronic methamphetamine abuse significantly alters brain function. Users exhibit reduced motor speed and impaired verbal learning. Recent studies of chronic methamphetamine abusers also revealed severe structural and functional changes in areas of the brain associated with emotion and memory, which may account for many of the emotional and cognitive problems observed in chronic methamphetamine abusers.

I talked recently with a woman who shared her history of meth addiction. One of the lucky ones, Maggie had used for only a year or so before having her children removed from her custody. Neighbors saw the users and dealers come and go while her children played in the yard unsupervised. Finally, Children's Protective Services took her children.

A single mother who is 28 but looks ten years older, Maggie still has circles under her eyes and sadness about the lost years.

"I'm just glad they [CPS] came when they did. Who knows what would have happened to me and my kids if they hadn't given me a wake-up call. Now I'm in recovery and have my kids back. Meth is a terrible drug. I did things I'll regret for the rest of my life when I was using. I lost my husband, lost my kids, lost my health, and lost my self-respect."

Maggie is one of the lucky ones. She's regaining her health. She still has the ability to hope and dream.

Methamphetamine users suffer endless consequences from their addiction. Not only does methamphetamine abuse create irritability, anxiety, confusion, and paranoia, but users become completely controlled by drug-seeking behavior. They absolutely must find their fix. In the meantime, their health erodes, their ability to care for their children and family slips away, and their relationships crumble.

Additionally, society is affected. These 2002 statistics are from the Bureau of Justice:

- Sixty-eight percent of jail inmates reported symptoms in the year before their admission to jail that met substance dependence or abuse criteria.

- Sixteen percent of convicted jail inmates said that they committed their offense to get money for drugs.

- Sixty-three percent of inmates who met substance dependence or abuse criteria had participated in substance treatment or other programs.

Working with recovering methamphetamine addicts is a heart-rending experience. Often having lost everything, they universally tell a story of focus on only one thing—finding their next high.

Hitting Bottom

Addictions of any kind inevitably lead to a serious breakdown in our lives. We simply cannot continue with addictive and compulsive behaviors without severe ramifications. We may be able to delay the consequences, but we can never fully avoid them.

Sooner or later we hit bottom, which becomes an opportunity for change. No breakthrough can happen without a breakdown, and that breakdown can be the best thing that ever happens to an addict. Although no one wants to experience the disorganization and loss that comes from a breakdown, this is often a powerful spiritual and emotional time of reconsideration.

E.M. Jellinek, a biostatistician, physiologist, and alcoholism researcher, is well-known for creating the Jellinek chart of addictions. His famous chart is used in most recovery programs to outline the horrific journey taken by so many addicts. (Elements from Jellinek's chart are used in the test included at the end of this chapter.)

With alcoholism and drugs, the downward spiral begins with these behaviors and symptoms:

- occasional relief drinking or drugging
- increasing dependence on alcohol or drugs
- concurrent feelings of guilt
- remorse and broken promises
- decreasing tolerance for alcohol
- impaired thinking
- unreasonable resentments
- indefinable fears and exhausted alibis

When many addicts hit bottom, they enter some form of recovery process where they seek help. They slowly begin to rebuild their lives in some treatment process and begin to...

- discontinue their drug or alcohol use
- develop a renewed physical, emotional, and spiritual life
- take stock of their life
- examine their destructive thinking
- develop healthy friendships
- think correctly and realistically
- experience a rise in self-esteem and emotional control
- experience a rebirth of their ideals

Though still working with CPS to ensure that she stays clean and sober, Maggie has discontinued her drug use. She attends church regularly and is reexamining her life. She is training to become a real estate agent and has discovered a newfound drive and ambition to succeed. She is not dating, stating that she wants to focus on her recovery, on being the best mother possible, and on creating a career for herself. She repeatedly says she is thankful for her harsh wake-up call because losing her children caused her to seek recovery.

The Bottom Line

Assessing the stories of alcoholics and drug addicts is challenging. Did they choose their addiction, or has their addiction chosen them? The line is blurred.

Alcoholics have myriad excuses for why they drink and why they do not seek treatment. Drug addicts have equally impaired reasoning, justifying their drug use in countless ways. I've sat with many recovering methamphetamine addicts who tell similar stories. Their early lives reflect a history of abuse and neglect, precursors to drug-seeking behaviors. They often began looking for a high in alcohol and then perhaps marijuana before they eventually "graduated" to methamphetamine.

All addicts begin with manageable lives, but somewhere they cross a line. Perhaps they begin with social drinking or a toke of marijuana. Their use gradually increases, oftentimes leading to heavier drugs. When they try meth, all bets are off. Once they reach this stage, they are absolutely controlled by their desire to get the drug.

Whether we subscribe to the notion that addictions are diseases, poor choices, genetic predispositions combined with social factors, or some combination, in the end we must take responsibility for our recovery. How we got here is less important than what we do now.

Spiritual Recovery

Every addiction leads to spiritual deterioration because addictions lead to the endless pursuit of something other than God. Regardless of how hard the addict tries to maintain balance, addiction leads to spiritual and sometimes physical death.

The Scriptures are clear on the matter. We are warned repeatedly about the dangers of alcohol and also about those people and things that would take our focus off our faith. We're cautioned to be on guard against anything that would enslave us. The apostle Paul tells us, "So then, let us not be like others, who are asleep, but let us be alert and self-controlled. For those who sleep, sleep at night, and those who get drunk, get drunk at night. But since we belong to the day, let us be self-controlled" (1 Thessalonians 5:6-8). The fruit of the Spirit includes self-control (Galatians 5:22).

We must take full responsibility for our addiction—how we got to where we are, how our lifestyle supports our addiction or our recovery, what we're doing to resolve the problem, and where we want to be in the future. Any recovery program must include the work of God in our lives.

In the pages ahead we'll explore other addictions and examine how they manifest themselves and what can be done about them.

Alcohol and Drug Addiction Test

This test will help you determine if you or someone you love has an alcohol or drug problem. The symptoms are adopted from the Jellinek chart. People who are not addicted do *not* experience the following problems.

If you have more than one or two affirmative answers, you have reason for concern. Three or more affirmative answers suggests a need for intervention in your life.

1. I use alcohol or drugs to get away from things that bother me. ❏ Yes ❏ No

2. I use alcohol or drugs to solve my problems.   ❏ Yes   ❏ No

3. I need more or stronger kinds of alcohol or drugs to produce the same feeling I used to get.   ❏ Yes   ❏ No

4. Sometimes after using I forget what happened.   ❏ Yes   ❏ No

5. Sometimes I hide my drinking or drug using from others.   ❏ Yes   ❏ No

6. I need alcohol or drugs to have fun.   ❏ Yes   ❏ No

7. Other people have complained about my drug or alcohol use.   ❏ Yes   ❏ No

8. I feel guilty about my drug or alcohol use.   ❏ Yes   ❏ No

9. I use problems in my life as an excuse to drink or use.   ❏ Yes   ❏ No

10. I feel bad about how my using hurts other people.   ❏ Yes   ❏ No

11. I make promises to change and then fail to do so.   ❏ Yes   ❏ No

12. I have made efforts in the past to change.   ❏ Yes   ❏ No

13. I try to control my drug or alcohol use.   ❏ Yes   ❏ No

14. I change jobs or relationships to make my life better.   ❏ Yes   ❏ No

15. My drug or alcohol use has caused health, legal, work, or relationship problems in my life.   ❏ Yes   ❏ No

16. I have experienced withdrawal symptoms.   ❏ Yes   ❏ No

17. I've said or done things I wouldn't   ❏ Yes   ❏ No
    normally do when using drugs
    or alcohol.

18. Drugs or alcohol have become   ❏ Yes   ❏ No
    a focus of my life.

CHAPTER SIX

Measuring Up

Once, during prohibition, I was forced to live
for days on nothing but food and water.

W.C. FIELDS

As I WRITE THIS CHAPTER I'm watching a television ad for a product that promises to reprogram your metabolism in six weeks or less. Remarkably, you'll lose fat fast without exercising. Further, the ad promises you can "lose weight anywhere."

For just four installments of $39.99, you'll receive a workbook, CDs, and even phone support that will ensure that you achieve your desired results. It's easy, it's inexpensive, and it works!

Fads of this type were discussed with enthusiasm in my family when I was growing up. My mom and three sisters were invariably intrigued by such offers. As you might imagine, they were very focused on appearances. Preparing for dances and dates and always concerned about fitting into the latest fashion, my sisters were always making sure they measured up. This invariably included losing weight, so my sisters were usually willing to try the latest diet.

I remember their excitement about the grapefruit diet. Studies had shown participants who ate half a grapefruit with each meal lost 3.6 pounds in a week. Those who drank one serving of grapefruit juice three times a day also lost several pounds.

I also remember the cabbage soup diet. This low-fat, high-fiber diet was particularly appealing because it lasted only seven days and was sure to kick-start serious weight loss. Like the grapefruit diet and all the others, it produced no significant results.

One sister even tried the ice cream diet, which touted "hot new research" revealing that ice cream, when part of a healthy diet, may actually melt away fat. Amazingly, this did not result in weight reduction. When I became an adult, I realized that my sisters and mother had been obsessed with measuring up because they live in a nation obsessed with measuring up.

All of this reinforces my position that we're a parade of addicts. None have escaped the clutches of some form of addictive or compulsive behavior. Those who believe otherwise are in denial— something we've learned is the hallmark of all addictions.

It's difficult to say which addiction is the most debilitating. Meth-amphetamine addiction gets a lot of press, and rightly so because of the way it ravages individuals and families. The press cite statistics about broken homes, neglected children, impoverished health, and hollow souls.

Others claim alcohol is the most dangerous predator. Citing deaths resulting from drunken driving, soaring costs due to absenteeism, liver disease, and the pain suffered by families of alcoholics and their victims, they too make a convincing argument.

What about nicotine addiction? Millions are addicted to smoking cigarettes and chewing tobacco. The tobacco industry is big business, and its livelihood depends on keeping addicted customers satisfied. The tobacco giants ask us to ignore nearly 44,000 deaths every year related to cigarette smoking.

And what about the onslaught of casinos and subsequent gambling addictions? I'm absolutely convinced that this problem will continue to gain public awareness in the coming years. Bingo parlors, casinos, backroom poker groups, and online betting are not simply forms of entertainment—they provide fertile ground for addiction.

Yet as momentous as these addictions are, another vies for top honors in the death-and-destruction department—addictions related to eating.

Anorexia, bulimia, and obesity are forms of food addiction. Kay Sheppard, in her book *Food Addiction,* states that "Food addicts are obsessed with food, preoccupied with weight and appearance and they experience progressive loss of control over the amount of food they eat."[1]

Consider the following statistics:

- Sixty percent of Americans are overweight. About a third are obese, which means they are more than 20 percent over ideal body weight.

- Obesity is a national health hazard, with untold millions of dollars spent in higher health insurance premiums. It complicates other health problems and adds to emotional disorders.

- One percent of teenage girls suffer from anorexia—an addiction related to the compulsive control of food—sometimes resulting in death.

- One percent of adult women suffer from binge eating and bulimia.

- About 2 percent of people suffer from body dysmorphic disorder, a mental disorder involving a distorted body image. It strikes males and females equally, usually before age 18.

As uncomfortable and awkward as we feel when these subjects are broached, we must talk about them. This chapter is devoted to our addictions to food and the consequences that follow: obesity, anorexia, and bulimia. We use laxatives to control weight, exercise fanatically to maintain our ideal of weight, and engage in other behaviors that reinforce these disorders. Food, and compulsive behaviors associated with it, causes immense personal, psychological, and physical problems.

Food Addiction

Kay Sheppard reminds us that food addicts aren't simply weak-willed or immoral, nor do they only have a bad habit or behavioral problem. She insists that a metabolic and biochemical component results in food addiction.

This is usually not our view of food addicts. We sometimes view obese or anorexic persons through the same shame-based lens we use with drug addicts—as people who have surrendered control of their lives. They just can't control themselves, we think. If they had stronger wills, they would be able to hit the gym like we do. If they had stronger temperaments, they would be able to eat just one cookie after dinner and let it go at that.

Not so, say the experts.

Food addicts are *obsessed* with recurring thoughts about buying, preparing, and eating food. They often are simply unable to stop eating.

Sheppard adds, "When a food addict loses control, it is like being driven at knifepoint to get and eat binge foods. There is an urgency which is never satisfied. That is the paradox of this addiction— addicts eat to feel better those foods which make them feel worse. The search for that one perfect bite is never over."[2]

Food addicts have often tried everything to manage their problem. Like the women in my family, they've embarked on endless diets, weight-loss programs, and special eating regimens, all to no avail. Over the years, efforts to control weight and eating fail repeatedly, adding to their malaise. They continually search for yet another pill, another diet, another calorie-counting routine or quick-fix formula to achieve the perfect weight they have conceived in their mind. The perfect formula, of course, is never found.

Like others in our parade of addicts, food addicts will remain sick until they overcome their denial. Denial keeps food addicts from seeking help. They use denial as others use denial—to maintain some semblance of normalcy in the midst of their sickness. Denial also enables them to avoid accurately naming the problem. The problem is not *only* that they have a biochemical predisposition to an eating disorder. Other confounding issues are often involved, such as a refusal to seek appropriate help for their problem. Denial keeps the individual locked in a dysfunctional pattern as opposed to seeking help through support groups, nutritional guidance, and healthy exercise regimens.

Secrecy

Secrecy is a central element of every addiction. In fact, we're only as sick as our secrets, according to Alcoholics Anonymous. The same is true of food addicts.

Although food addiction is often obvious, especially in cases involving obesity, a great deal of secrecy surrounds the problem. Food addicts, such as bulimics, anorexics, laxative users, and binge eaters, live secret lives.

Jenny, who is 44, has been in counseling with me for more than a year for recurring bouts of depression. Moderately obese, Jenny has a broad smile and short brown hair and dresses fashionably. She works full-time in a bank, thoroughly enjoys her work, and receives many accolades for her performance. She is happily married with two grown sons. She is also a perfectionist, and that trait sometimes causes problems for her.

Jenny generally manages her depression and has worked hard to discover the triggers that sometimes sneak up on her. She's found that work stress can lead to fatigue and then excessive eating.

Although she might occasionally slip into a depression lasting several weeks, more often she identifies her difficulties, works on them, and quickly returns to her high level of functioning.

Jenny and her husband, Stan, are active in their church. Jenny plays the piano for worship, and Stan teaches a Sunday school class. They enjoy their life and take frequent vacations to Southern California to visit their kids.

Things had been going very well until a recent incident sent Jenny spiraling downward. She came to her weekly session unusually distressed.

"I'm not doing well," Jenny said tearfully, wringing her hands.

"What's happened?" I asked.

"I'm obsessed with losing weight again. In fact, I'm embarrassed to tell you what I've done."

Jenny's eyes darted around the room as she struggled to manage her anxiety.

"What is it, Jenny?" I asked.

"I've been using laxatives again," she said, starting to sob. "I haven't been completely honest with you in the past. I've used laxatives and even some of my husband's diuretics. I'm just so desperate to lose weight."

"It took a lot of courage to tell me this, and that's a great first step. Have you told Stan yet?"

"No," she said. "He'd be so disappointed. He thought I was over this. I hate myself at times like this. I hate sneaking food, throwing up, and taking laxatives. But they help me lose weight and make me feel better."

I was surprised to hear this. I knew Jenny's history included an eating disorder, that she had struggled to lose weight in the past and had even attended an eating disorder support group years ago.

"The next step is to tell Stan," I said.

"I'm not ready to do that. And I don't want to give up the laxatives. They make me feel better."

"I understand your desire to manage this yourself, Jenny, but it's reached a point where keeping it a secret will work against you. By telling Stan, you'll gain his support."

Jenny and I spent that session and the following one talking about her eating disorder. She was 50 pounds overweight and very frightened about her compulsive behaviors. She was caught in a vicious downward spiral of binging and using laxatives and diuretics to maintain her weight, but she refused to join a weight-loss program that might help her reach her goal in a healthier, more effective way.

Jenny is typical of millions of people, often women, caught in the throes of attempting to achieve a nearly impossible self-image that is often 50 to 150 pounds less than their current weight. They're caught in cycles of binging, purging, dieting, and obsession over their favorite foods. Their moods yo-yo as abruptly as their weight, adding to the problem.

Even in the midst of her weight challenges, Jenny was able to reinvigorate her spiritual life. She ultimately participated in a support group at her church, where she was able to take responsibility for her behavior. She quit her use of laxatives after becoming accountable to her husband. Gradually she claimed God's promise, spoken by the psalmist David: "I praise you because I am fearfully and wonderfully made; your works are wonderful, I know that full well. My frame was not hidden from you when I was made in the secret place. When I was woven together in the depths of the earth, your eyes saw my unformed body" (Psalm 139:14).

Cravings

Like most addicts, Jenny feels bad about her secretive behavior, and she feels embarrassed and ashamed that she cannot control herself. She believes she is weak-willed and unable to resist her cravings. Her secretive behavior escalates, and soon she's completely out of control. As we've seen, we're only as sick as our secrets, so remaining quiet about what's going on in our heads and bodies is a sure way to increase the power of our addiction.

Jenny knows what many others don't—that her body craves certain foods. Non-addicted people can stop eating when they have had enough, but food addicts never get enough. They are never satisfied with moderate amounts of food, so they continue to eat well past normal satiation. They don't just *want* to have another helping of potatoes, they *crave* another plateful.

Food addicts are similar to alcoholics, who crave another drink, or drug addicts who crave their next marijuana or methamphetamine high. When food addicts put food into their bodies, they experience out-of-control hunger. At this point, the body craves more of the same food. Like other addicts, food addicts must identify their "trigger" foods to determine what initially caused the cravings and then abstain from those in the future.

Food cravings have been shown to be related to low blood sugar or low serotonin, another feel-good neurotransmitter. The brain issues a signal that it needs a pick-me-up, and the cravings begin. This signal often causes a sugar or carbohydrate craving that, when sated, offers the addict a short burst of serotonin. The addict feels good for a moment, only to return to the low-serotonin state, activating the cravings again.

Again we ask, does the food addict choose the addiction, or does the addiction choose the addict? The answer may forever remain unclear.

Barbie Doll Syndrome

Society does very little to help the food addict. Passing through the grocery counter, you'll see a dozen magazine covers with images of perfect bodies that America idolizes. We adore the celebrity who is perfectly proportioned, perhaps even a bit underweight. The blonde bombshell has a gorgeous man on her arm, and the message is clear: If you have the perfect body, the perfect skin, the perfect hairstyle, you too can have the perfect man and the perfect life.

Deep down, we know this message is bunk. We read the stories of the celebrity's short journey into stardom, followed by the long journey into alcohol, drugs, and eating disorders. Still, we are pummeled with images of the beautiful starlet, teased into believing this life can be achieved by all. Drs. Jim Kirkpatrick and Paul Caldwell, in their book *Eating Disorders,* comment on the influence these images have on young women in our society:

> The "ideal" female in Western media is exceptionally tall and abnormally thin, which is a state very few women can achieve...It's a seductive process; thinness and beauty promise many things. You will be respected, more successful, sexier, we are told. You will look more confident, be more self-assured, have more self-esteem. The ideal supposedly confers power, youthfulness and a sense of being in control.[3]

These authors refer to the "Barbie doll syndrome," noting that the Barbie doll is one of the most successful toys ever conceived, with over 800 million Barbie dolls sold worldwide and sales topping $1 billion. The problem is that many young girls believe Barbie's proportions to be realistic and attainable—which is not true. Barbie is thinner than normal, with a larger bust and longer legs than would be normal for someone her size. There is a huge discrepancy between the body proportions of healthy, normal women and the proportions of these ubiquitous dolls. When the dolls are used as standards, the result can be discontent and even despair.

Bombarded by celebrities' publicity photos and stories, which we cannot seem to get enough of, we turn to books about the latest, greatest diets. You too can achieve your perfect goal for your perfect weight for your perfect look, they tell us. Most of these fad diets, however, are dangerously unbalanced, leading again to feelings of discouragement and possibly even poor health.

Society's Contradictions

Back at the grocery checkout, we move past the magazines with the images of Hollywood's most glamorous women and men, and next we come to rows and rows of high-fat, high-calorie candy bars—impulse foods that few can resist.

Amazing!

We're teased into believing we can look like Angelina Jolie, Brad Pitt, George Clooney, or Jessica Simpson. At the same time, we're enticed to indulge in our favorite junk food. We're bludgeoned with contradictory messages that lead many of us into food schizophrenia. We're supposed to look great and weigh the perfect weight while indulging in the addictive delicacies of junk food.

Not long ago Bill Gates traveled to Omaha, Nebraska. He and Warren Buffett went out together for lunch—to McDonald's! Both men love burgers. Eating out, American style, is part of their ritual when together. When we see powerful or beautiful people enjoying the same foods we crave, we rationalize that eating this way must be okay. Tempting fast-food establishments are within blocks anytime.

McDonald's now operates more than 28,000 restaurants around the world. They are America's biggest buyer of beef, pork, and potatoes. One in eight American workers has been employed by the fast-food behemoth. You can't go more than a few blocks in any city without spotting those ubiquitous golden arches.

Who doesn't love McDonald's Big Mac or their Quarter Pounder with cheese? I'm hungry just thinking about it. Yes, of course we can eat every meal of the day there, but as Eric Schlosser noted in his book *Fast Food Nation,* we'll soon be packing around more pounds because of it.

This is the simple truth: We can't eat regularly at fast-food establishments without becoming overweight. We can't grab a candy bar every time we rush through the grocery line and expect to remain healthy. We must slow down, not only in our pace of life but also in the way we approach food, if we want to be healthy. In the process, we can expect little support from society.

Obesity

We're an overweight nation. In fact, studies indicate we're getting fatter and fatter every year. Some believe this is related to our hectic lifestyle and the ease with which we can drive through and grab a meal. More and more adults and children are obese, and obesity in children is a strong predictor of obesity in adulthood.

Obesity, defined as being 20 percent or more above ideal body weight, affects a person's general well-being and quality of life. An obese person typically feels constantly tired and is unable to be active because of shortness of breath, joint pain (especially in the knees and the back), and other ills. It can also result in decreased productivity because of absenteeism brought about by various illnesses.

Although society generally ignores obesity, obese individuals live in their own inner torment. They know how uncomfortable they feel when shopping for clothes, when being seated in an auditorium, or when ordering in a restaurant. They know the embarrassment of socializing with others who are thinner, the humiliation of swimming in a hotel pool, and the terror that accompanies intimate activities. They can never climb outside the skin that always reminds them that they don't measure up.

Much confusion surrounds obesity, with many factors contributing to this personal and societal problem. Obesity is primarily an addiction to food. But obesity is also an addiction to a lifestyle that promotes eating at fast-food restaurants and avoiding exercise. This is often compounded by a hereditary predisposition to excessive weight gain.

Clear physiological issues are connected to obesity, such as having excessive fat cells that are not easily absorbed. As people gradually gain weight, they increase the size of their fat cells. They can lose weight but may not necessarily rid themselves of the fat cells, making it even more difficult to keep the pounds off.

There is also the set point theory. Drs. Kirkpatrick and Caldwell note that the human body is programmed to be a specific weight at certain ages. "The set point theory of weight states that, like our height, eye color and intelligence, our weight is genetically determined. Although we can increase or decrease it to some degree, it will always tend to return to its predetermined level. This is one of the reasons weight-loss diets have a failure rate over 95 percent."[4]

Having worked with hundreds of obese individuals, I believe that many factors perpetuate obesity.

- Genetic predisposition: Clearly some predisposing factors lead to obesity, and these must be acknowledged and respected.
- Lack of exercise: Many are simply unwilling or unable to maintain consistent aerobic exercise.
- Fast-food lifestyle: Many persist in eating fast food and don't engage in slow dining or cooking at home.
- Trigger foods: Many don't respect and abstain from their trigger foods, which are often high in sugar and carbohydrates.
- Sedentary lifestyle: Many spend an excessive amount of time in front of the television and computer instead of burning calories.
- High-calorie snacks: Many snacks include high sugar and fat content and contribute significantly to weight gain.
- Lack of commitment to proper weight loss: Many people with problems refuse to participate in support groups to assist them in a recovery process.

The data are clear—food addictions have serious ramifications and are difficult to treat. Physiological, cultural, societal, familial, and even personal hurdles challenge those who try to work effectively with this addiction.

If you struggle with obesity, recovery must involve a clear and determined focus. Like the alcoholic or drug addict, you must stop at nothing to find a recovery process that works for you. Most experts agree that recovery from obesity involves healthy eating, exercise, avoidance of trigger foods, support, and an active lifestyle.

Anorexia

The world of food addicts is comprised of those who cannot stop from binging on their favorite foods, those who binge and then purge, and those who cannot force themselves to eat at all.

I vividly recall working several years ago with a 13-year-old girl named Katie. She was strong-willed and somewhat angry. She was a contrast in appearances, with the body of a waif from a refugee camp and the defiant expression of a boxer. She didn't want to be in counseling and felt threatened by therapists and a physician who told her to gain weight or risk being hospitalized. Obviously at least 20 pounds underweight, Katie appeared gaunt and tired. With dark pools under her eyes and hollow cheeks, she looked sad even when talking about her active social life. She had only a superficial understanding of her problem.

This case was no small challenge. Katie was dangerously underweight and was being monitored closely by her physician, who mandated that she eat a certain number of calories daily. Katie didn't want to gain weight and went along with the plan only because of the threat of hospitalization—a fate that awaits many anorexics.

Anorexia is characterized by the following symptoms:

- refusal to maintain or achieve 85 percent of the expected body weight for the person's age and height
- intense fear of gaining weight or becoming fat
- distorted view of body image, with excessive importance placed on weight and appearance

- denial of being underweight, despite overwhelming evidence to the contrary
- amenorrhea—the absence of at least three consecutive menstrual cycles

Anorexia can strike any age group, but the majority of victims are adolescents. Kids at this age are especially susceptible to cultural emphases on thinness, they experience unusual emotional swings, and they often struggle with self-image, which includes weight. Anorexics are often obsessed with control—they discover that they can lose weight, which is very important to them, and thus their control becomes self-reinforcing, leading to severe dieting.

Katie, like many other anorexics, was a perfectionist and high achiever. She expected nothing but A's in school and mercilessly punished herself if she didn't live up to her lofty standards. She studied compulsively, exercised compulsively, and ruled her emotions with the same demanding spirit.

Anorexia is a complicated mixture of emotional, psychological, and physical symptoms. Sadly, what often starts out as a simple diet plan leads to an obsession with losing weight. The weight loss doesn't stop at a reasonable goal, but rather continues to a life-threatening level.

Katie was a typical anorexic. She was the third child of middle-class parents, with high-achieving older siblings. Her older sisters were college graduates and were also good-looking. Katie felt competitive, wanting to be like them. Her obsession with good looks and perfection spiraled out of control.

Katie didn't want to be hospitalized and was willing to talk about conflicts she was experiencing with her parents. Beneath her distorted body image and facade of control, she struggled with low self-esteem and a fiercely competitive spirit. As she worked on her self-esteem in counseling and learned about the severity of her problem, Katie was willing to get better, though this was a minor concession at first. After a while, she gained weight, felt better physically, and was able to express emotions in healthier ways. Gradually, she returned to a healthier life and lifestyle, though she also understood that she would always have to guard against taking this route again.

Not all anorexics are as fortunate as Katie. Some fight to maintain control of their weight to the point of death. Some, especially runners and gymnastic athletes, become obsessed not only with their weight but also with exercise, working out to the point of absurdity. Many must learn that balance is the key.

If you or someone you love struggles with anorexia, obtaining immediate professional help is critically important. Anorexia is a serious emotional and physical disorder, with consequences that can be life-threatening.

Bulimia

Many people attempt to control their weight through the inappropriate use of vomiting, laxatives, diuretics, suppositories, and enemas. These are desperate measures by desperate people in an attempt to manage their weight.

Bulimics want to eat and often do so by binging, but they also want to rid themselves of the calories that accompany eating. As with other food addicts, they use secretive behaviors, rationalizations, and justifications to continue their actions. All the while, they feel completely out of control beneath their cool facade.

Bulimia carries serious consequences. The use of laxatives, persistent vomiting, and the use of diuretics leaves the body depleted of necessary nutrients and minerals. Repeated vomiting leads to a sore or damaged throat and an acidic stomach. Sometimes the force of repeated vomiting causes broken blood vessels around the eyes, and the teeth and gums often show permanent damage.

Bulimics falsely believe they can maintain proper body weight through their desperate measures. This is rarely true, and as with other addictions, their behavior often leads to more severe psychological, physical, and spiritual problems.

Emotional Eating

Food addictions create emotional problems, and emotional problems intensify the addictions. Recovery from the addictions must incorporate various aspects of emotional healing.

Food addiction specialists agree that recovery must involve an understanding of how, where, when, and with whom you feel most vulnerable to your compulsive behaviors. It is critical to recognize and fully understand your emotional triggers.

Jenny has struggled courageously with her bulimia and has learned in counseling that she had been pushing herself too hard without a vacation. She had been tiring more easily, had stopped exercising on a regular basis, and had been slowly gaining weight. Anxiety about her appearance, along with her history of mild depression, was an emotional trigger leading to her relapse into bulimia. She slipped into old behaviors of using laxatives and vomiting to manage her feelings and her weight.

Although Katie is recovering from her anorexia, she must be vigilant about her emotional health. She must guard against unrealistic expectations, undue competitiveness, and family power struggles.

Like other food addicts, Jenny and Katie must watch closely for the following symptoms:

- stress, tension, and anxiety
- depression and mood fluctuations
- fatigue
- lack of play and recreational opportunities
- feelings of rejection
- suppressed anger, bitterness, and resentment
- lack of support and appreciation
- lack of spiritual support and accountability

Path to Perfection

Food addicts are tangled in an ongoing struggle to become someone other than who they are. Aside from hereditary complications, food addictions are often attempts to manage uncomfortable feelings. In many cases, they are vain strategies to become perfect. In the end, addicts wind up being *less* perfect. They become slaves to their compulsive behaviors.

Someone has said, "The way to be perfect is to be perfectly you."

No one has walked your path. No one has gone through the struggles you've gone through. No one has experienced the losses and victories you've experienced. There is no one like you.

The psalmist says much about how God views us. David seems to truly understand that he is loved and cared for by God. He says, "I call on you, O God, for you will answer me; give ear to me and hear my prayer…Keep me as the apple of your eye; hide me in the shadow of your wings" (Psalm 17:6,8).

David repeatedly seeks God's protection and provision, but we always sense that he believes God delights in him.

Wherever you are today, with whatever addictions you have in your life, know that God loves you and is faithfully committed to you.

CHAPTER SEVEN

Sexual Sanity

Can a man scoop fire into his lap without his clothes being burned?
Can a man walk on hot coals without his feet being scorched?
So is he who sleeps with another man's wife;
no one who touches her will go unpunished.

PROVERBS 6:27-29

S-E-X.

I thought I could approach this topic with ease, but I can't. Even though I work with individuals and couples experiencing sexual problems, I still get uneasy just talking about the subject.

And I feel guilty about feeling uneasy. I'm 56 years old and married, and I believe I'm sexually normal. Still, early years of silence and embarrassment have left their impression. A society that offers only a twisted, sensationalized view of sexuality hasn't helped either. I still blush when the topic is mentioned.

Perhaps you're the same. You may struggle to distinguish between healthy and unhealthy sexuality, and to know where to draw the line when talking about sexual addiction. But first, let's discuss what sexuality has to do with sanity.

Sexuality is a natural part of our being and includes our erotic feelings, our sexual fantasies, and of course, our sexual actions. These actions include far more than intercourse and have much to do with how we feel about ourselves, what we find sexually appealing, and the boundaries we create to keep ourselves sexually safe.

Most of us learned about the mechanics of sexuality from friends, the media, or family. But we often don't know much about what healthy sexuality really looks like.

Wendy Maltz, in her book *Incest and Sexuality,* lists five traits necessary for healthy sexuality:

- *Consent.* Both partners are able to say what they like and dislike in their sexual relationship and respect each other's feelings.
- *Equality.* Each partner feels equal to the other and does not feel coerced, overpowered, or threatened in any way.
- *Respect.* Each partner feels respected and treats the other with complete respect.
- *Trust.* Both partners can trust themselves and their mate.
- *Safety.* Both partners feel safe with each other.

This list gives us a foundation for talking about healthy sexuality, but we need to know and practice much more. We must bring healthy attitudes as well as healthy behaviors to our sexual relationship, including these:

- *Passion.* Each of us wants to be desired, to be found attractive, to be pursued.

- *Romance.* Each of us wants to be romanced, to be "wined and dined." A sexual relationship void of romance is a chain of mechanical acts.

- *Affection.* We all want to be shown affection, to be touched in sexual and nonsexual ways that are unique to us.

- *Commitment.* We want to know our mate will be there when the passion fires burn and when they've receded.

- *Intimacy.* We need "into me see" to enjoy a healthy sexual relationship.

- *Sensuality.* We need to be aware of our own sensuality, including our body image and feelings, as well as how and where we want to be touched.

- *Eroticism.* We must know what is erotic for us and what is erotic for our mate, and we need to make sexual decisions accordingly.

Contrast this information with the magazine ads bombarding us at the checkout counter. Much of society seems not to care much about respect in relationships or about creating a sanctuary of safety and trust for sexuality. The importance of stability and commitment in a relationship as a requirement for trust and safety is frequently ignored.

While working out at the gym, I perused a magazine and discovered that if I purchased a TiVo, I could be assured of having a beautiful, sensuous blonde on my arm. If I drank a certain microbrew, women would swarm to me like bees to honey. If I drove a Porsche convertible, I'd be inundated with more ladies than I could handle.

The media assaults us with distorted sexual images. Stunning men and women parade across our television screens. Scantily clad females invade our consciousness from every possible angle at every possible opportunity. Nowhere, however, do we hear about trust, respect, equality, commitment, romance, or intimacy.

Rarely do we hear about God's plan for sexuality, which involves sensuality within the confines and safety of marriage. Rarely do we hear about the joys of sexuality within the committed and caring embrace of your mate. We're left to sort these things out on our own.

Sexual Addiction

In too many lives, sexuality enslaves. Sexual addiction occurs when sexual thoughts and behaviors become compulsive, controlling us and turning our behavior into unequal, disrespecting relationships. Sexual addiction involves objectifying others or engaging in hurtful behavior that leads to the degradation of ourselves and our marriage. Sexual addiction is characterized by shameful, secretive behaviors that often lead to riskier behaviors. Like other addicts, sexual addicts deny the severity of their problem, justifying their actions or minimizing the impact it has on others. They have a strong need to make their behavior seem normal and refuse to admit that they are addicted or that they need help.

Sexual addiction progresses much like other addictions. Sex addicts are typically not content with one form of sexual expression, but take greater and greater risks in spite of negative consequences. They usually stop or seek help only after getting caught in their addiction. And even if caught, they often return to their previous behavior patterns.

Behaviors associated with sexual addiction include these:

- compulsive masturbation (self-stimulation)
- multiple affairs
- multiple or anonymous sexual partners and one-night stands
- constant viewing of pornography
- unsafe sex

- phone and computer sex (cybersex)
- solicitation of prostitutes
- exhibitionism
- compulsive dating through personal ads
- voyeurism and stalking
- sexual harassment
- molestation and rape

For those caught up in the world of sexual perversion and addiction, risky sexual behavior creates the same serotonin and dopamine highs we've talked about, creating further chaos and self-destructive behavior. The spiral continues downward until some crisis brings everything to a stop.

The Garden

Sex and sanity were quite compatible in the beginning. You'll recall that God made Adam and then decided it wasn't good for Adam to be alone. Rather than creating a hunting buddy, a tennis partner, or a jogging pal, He created a life partner, Eve.

The Scriptures tell us Adam said, "This is now bone of my bones and flesh of my flesh; she shall be called 'woman,' for she was taken out of man" (Genesis 2:23).

I like to think that Adam became enraptured with the thought of someone who would share his deepest thoughts, feel his most intense emotions, and share a journey together, which included healthy sexuality. I imagine Adam being curious about this beautiful woman, excited to discover how she thought, and what she appreciated. And yes, I imagine that he was attracted to her sensuality. Together they would share physical pleasures as an expression of their emotional and spiritual intimacy.

Imagine. They are living in the most beautiful place on earth. We're told that the garden was filled with trees that were "pleasing to the eye and good for food" (Genesis 2:9). Springs flowed from the ground, and a river flowed through the garden. The place was paradise.

And they lived in innocence, naked and unashamed. Sex and sanity dwelled happily and peacefully together—for a time.

In the Genesis account, sin entered the world, and sexuality became soiled. Every aspect of creation, including our sexuality, was created in purity. But the fall of humankind brought corruption. In the context of selfishness, immaturity, and greed, we became takers instead of givers. We came to treat sex as something to get instead of something we lovingly create together. We stopped treating one another with equality, respect, and trust, and in the process, we damaged our sexual relationships.

Nevada Street

Writing this chapter has forced me to consider my own life and my own sexual identity. I look back at my sexual beginning, when I thought my sex interests could not be controlled or contained. Seemingly overnight, I became obsessed with girls, completely objectifying them.

Raised in the small, sleepy town of Bellingham, Washington, just south of the Canadian border in the Pacific Northwest, I lived on a small street with lots of playmates. That's what they were for the longest time—playmates.

And then adolescence hit like a blast of TNT. Suddenly, with hormones raging, the guys I played sports with talked more about girls than athletics. Their language became overtly sexual as they shared explicit stories and explicit pictures. Girls I had innocently played with became objects of curiosity and possible conquest. I noticed my development and their development, and I felt obsessed with thoughts about sex.

Sometimes I felt God had played a cruel joke on me. I had these powerful sexual impulses but understood very little about them. No adult ever shared accurate information about the subject with me, so I struggled to learn all I could from my buddies, never wanting to appear uninformed about such important matters. Caught up in ignorance, embarrassment, and curiosity, I was confused about how one dealt with such powerful impulses.

As my buddies began to talk about sexual encounters and conquests, sorting out fact from fiction became more and more difficult. I considered the possibility of seeking out a sexually active life, but decided that wasn't appropriate for me because of my spiritual upbringing. I'd been taught that sex was something to be saved for marriage. I felt compelled by my spiritual beliefs to remain chaste until marriage.

I noticed sexual language in every locker room. Television and movies included sexual innuendos or graphic images. Explicit magazines began circulating, adding fuel to the fire. Every interaction over the next five years seemed to have some element of sexuality in it. Flirtation, sexual language, graphic images—all were emotional hits to my brain, causing me to go back for more, causing me to wonder about my own emerging sexuality.

Inching my way through adolescence, I realized God wasn't playing a cruel joke. All adolescents struggle with the same impulses. Just as God expected Adam and Eve to enjoy Eden but not to violate boundaries, so He created a vast and wonderful garden in the form of our sexuality and expects us to maintain healthy boundaries.

Violation of Boundaries

With such strong impulses, maintaining healthy boundaries is challenging. God knows we have desires that can quickly turn into compulsions. He created us as sensual and sexual people, with the ability to enjoy one another. However, a good thing can turn bad almost instantly. He knows our temptations and set guidelines for us to follow so we can live meaningful lives. When Adam and Eve stepped outside those guidelines, the results were catastrophic.

The apostle Paul offers repeated instructions about sexual behavior. In his letter to the Corinthian church, he repeatedly warns about sexual immorality, noting that since we have been united spiritually with Christ, immoral sexual actions defile our relationship to Him: "The body is not meant for sexual immorality, but for the Lord, and the Lord for the body...Do you not know that your body is a temple of the Holy Spirit?" (1 Corinthians 4:13,19).

Repeated immoral actions become habitual and turn into rituals, which become self-reinforcing. Consistently violating boundaries often leads to sexual addiction. How can we determine whether we are addicted to sex? Patrick Carnes, a leading authority on sexual addiction, enlightens us in his book *Don't Call It Love*.

> People ask how sex can be an addiction. It is not like a drug or alcohol which is foreign to the body...We have learned that addictive obsession can exist in whatever generates significant mood alteration, whether it be the self-nurturing of food, the excitement of gambling, or the arousal of seduction. One of the more destructive parts of sex addiction is that you literally carry your own source of supply.[1]

Like other addictions, sexual addiction is characterized by two key features: Addicts cannot control a particular behavior, and they continue that behavior despite significant harmful consequences. Thus, even if a person's sexual behavior isn't discovered for a long while, he or she may still have a sexual addiction.

Sexual addictions are often revealed in situations like these:

- Your spouse discovers a cache of pornography on your computer.
- You've been caught in your third adulterous affair.
- You've been fired from your job because of an inappropriate sexual liaison you were warned about and knew was wrong.
- You've been arrested for sexual behavior with minors.

- You engage in riskier and riskier sexual behavior without regard for the consequences.
- You're caught in an adult bookstore, leaving you feeling embarrassed and humiliated.

In his book *Addicted to Love,* Stephen Arterburn writes about what comprises a sexual addiction and how it is differentiated from healthy sexuality. He cites the following characteristics of a sexual addiction:

- Addictive sex is often done in isolation and is devoid of relationship. The sexual behavior is detached and isolated from other people.
- Addictive sex is sex for its own sake rather than for the mutual gratification of two people.
- The partner isn't really a person but an object to be used for sexual gratification.
- Addictive sex is devoid of intimacy. Sex addicts are utterly self-focused. They cannot achieve genuine intimacy because their self-obsession leaves no room for giving to others.
- Addictive sex victimizes others. It is self-gratifying. Addicts have little regard for the harmful effects of their behavior on others or themselves.
- Addictive sex ends in despair. When married couples make love, they're more fulfilled for having had the experience. Addictive sex leaves the participants feeling guilty, regretting the experience.
- Addictive sex is used to escape pain and problems. As with other addictions, sexual addiction is progressive, leading to increasingly degrading behavior.[2]

Sexual Beginnings

How does one become a sexual addict? How does something that feels so good turn into something so bad? Like other addictions, sexual addiction often has its roots early in childhood and family history. Although correlations are far from definitive, many sexual addicts grow up in chaotic, hostile, or neglectful homes. Other addictions, such as alcoholism, are often present. Many addicts are introduced to sexuality at an early age, with some experts believing that a high percentage of sexual addicts were sexually abused themselves in childhood.

We are just now becoming aware of the high rates of childhood sexual molestation. Not that long ago, we believed that only females were abuse victims. Many now believe that at least as many as one out of every five boys will have been abused by the time he turns 18. One out of every three females will suffer the same fate.

People who are hurting often hurt other people! Sexual addicts, having been victimized themselves, learn how to victimize. Having been objectified, they learn how to objectify others. Having dulled themselves to their inner pain, they lack empathy for others and do not sense the pain they cause.

Sexual addicts were often raised in an environment where sexual pleasure was associated not only with excitement but also with shame. Thus, anything exhilarating was also shameful. When the child grows up, he may be turned on by sex in high-risk situations and require riskier and riskier sexual encounters to produce the same high.

Families that struggle with myriad addictions, that violate boundaries, and that cloud sexuality in shame and secrecy provide the perfect environment for sexual addiction to develop.

The Secret Addiction

Sexual addiction may be the most secretive addiction. Many are willing to admit to abusing alcohol or drugs before admitting to their sexual cravings, which they perceive as shameful.

We've only begun to study and learn about sexual addictions. They have been hidden from society, so we've only recently begun talking about them openly. Now that we're talking, however, we're discovering sexual addiction in all levels of our society. In fact, we're becoming anesthetized because we've heard so much recently about political and even religious leaders with sexual addictions. Anne Wilson Schaef says this in her book *Escape from Intimacy*:

> Sexual addiction is a hidden addiction; I have found more willingness to confront almost any other addiction. Sexual addiction carries a particularly large component of shame and denial with it. Paradoxically, it is also one of the addictions that is most integrated into our society as "normal." It is only as the courageous persons with this addiction have come forth and named their addiction that we have been able to see the pervasiveness of this disease and the extent of the pain and suffering associated with it.[3]

Kyle, a tall, muscular man with wavy red hair, was referred to me by his pastor. Only 32 years old, he and his wife, Kelly, had been married for seven years and had two young daughters.

Kyle sat deep in his chair, looking sheepishly at me during our first session.

"What brings you in?" I said, noting that he had left blank the space on the form asking the reason for the counseling visit.

"My wife thinks I need to be here," he answered cautiously.

"Why does your wife think you need to be here?"

Kyle paused, appearing even more tense. "I travel a lot," he said. "I have a problem with women when I travel out of town. My wife caught me again and is devastated. I've hurt her so badly this time that she may be done with me."

Kyle's presentation was halting, and he seemed notably saddened.

"This is hard for you, isn't it?" I asked.

"Definitely," he said. "I never thought I'd be seeing a shrink. And I never thought my sex life would control me the way it does. I don't mean to hurt her, and I keep promising myself that it's going to stop."

"Tell me more about your problem."

"This is very personal and private stuff," he said. "I'm ashamed of what I do. Your sex life isn't something you share with a stranger."

"I can understand that," I said. "We're taught not to talk about our sexuality with others, especially strangers. I'll bet it was even hard to talk to Pastor Steve about this."

"Christians shouldn't struggle with this stuff," he said. "It's disgusting when I think about it. But I've always been real sexual," he said. "My wife isn't, and I can't seem to talk to her about it. So I've developed this secret life that's not so secret anymore. My wife always catches me cheating on her, and now she's done. If I don't get help, she says she'll divorce me. I don't really blame her."

"Sex can be just as addictive as drugs," I said. "We dabble with it, thinking we're in control. But like drugs, pretty soon we've got this double life, and we're doing things we never thought we'd ever do."

"You've got me pegged," he said, sighing heavily. "I'm ashamed of myself. I'd like to think it's in the past now, but I've said that before."

"How many times have you cheated on her?" I asked.

Kyle was slow to respond.

"A lot. I can't count how many. But I think I've learned a lesson, and hope it's in the past."

"Maybe it is in the past, or maybe it will come back to bite you in the backside. It's certainly not in the past for your wife. Maybe if we talk about this we can figure out what's going on."

It took some time, but Kyle eventually opened up. I've worked with many men like him who were able to brag in the locker room about their sexual exploits but who were also highly self-conscious when it came to actually admitting troubling behavior.

Over the next several weeks, Kyle shared more about his serial affairs. He minimized his behavior at first, but gradually he told me about keeping women's names and numbers on his cell phone and conducting several ongoing affairs that were devoid of sincere relationship. He admitted to visiting adult bookstores and even one group sexual experience, which his wife still doesn't know about. Though he'd been caught before and stopped his behavior for a time, he always slipped back into old patterns.

Kyle's wife, Kelly, came to see me a short time later. A tall woman with warm, gentle features, she was notably shaken by her husband's actions. Crying profusely at times, she told me that she couldn't understand why Kyle kept cheating on her. She had tried to forgive him, but each time she caught him her trust was broken and the gulf between them widened. Devastated and enraged over his most recent relapse, she insisted he receive counseling if she was going to stay in the marriage.

Although Kyle was moved by her pain, he offered few explanations for his behavior, other than their inability to talk about their sexual relationship. Kelly became angrier when he implied she might be part of the reason for his actions.

Kyle was clearly caught up in an addictive cycle, much like that described by Carnes. Feeling rejected by his wife and unwilling to talk about those feelings, he acted out his frustrations through repeated affairs. Soon he had developed a ritualized pattern that produced a powerful high. He had his routine—a woman in each part of the country to which he traveled.

Having hit bottom, Kyle truly wanted to save his marriage and to stop his sexual addiction. Coming out of the shadows was the first powerful step toward healing. His path, however, would be more arduous than either he or his wife imagined. He had well-entrenched rituals, and he wouldn't be able to walk away from his addictive patterns as easily as he hoped. It would require commitment, accountability, and complete honesty—including honesty with his wife.

Greener Grass

Even as we struggle to be satisfied with our marriage relationships, advertisements challenge our senses with the possibility that the grass is greener on the other side of the fence. More beautiful women or more handsome men are available if we simply reach out for them. Others are happier, we believe, and so we begin our search.

Believing that we can find someone better who will meet our needs is one of our greatest temptations, and it is actively promoted by our culture. This is, of course, simply a variation on the "forbidden fruit" theme in the garden—"you can eat of any of these trees except for this one." We're always wondering what other experiences might hold for us. Drug addicts share stories of always pursuing a higher high.

Even though Adam and Eve had everything they could want, they reached for more, not unlike us. This is the way we are with sexuality. We scan the horizon for something or someone better across the way.

Sexual addiction, as with other addictions, is about wanting more. It's about not being satisfied with what we have and searching for something more to fill an empty place in our soul.

Remember, any addict wants a chemical high, obtained either through the use of illicit substances or an experience (sexual or otherwise) that alters the dopamine or serotonin levels in the brain. Sexual acting out creates such a brain chemical experience, which leads to craving more and more of that experience.

The apostle John says, "For everything in the world—the cravings of sinful man, the lust of the eyes and the boasting of what he has and does—comes not from the Father but from the world" (1 John 2:16). This is a root cause of sexual addictions—craving more.

Let's consider some of the sexual experiences that can become addicting.

Pornography

For some people, sexually explicit images are extremely addictive. With these images readily available in the privacy of our homes through the portals of the Internet, addiction to pornography is increasing. Men especially struggle with pornographic addictions, though more women seem to be dabbling in this arena.

Jesus had strong words about our sexual thoughts and behaviors. He said, "You have heard that it was said, 'Do not commit adultery.' But I tell you that anyone who looks at a woman lustfully has already committed adultery with her in his heart" (Matthew 5:27).

Why did Jesus take such a strong stand against lust? He knew that when people lustfully view pornography, nakedness, and explicit sexual displays, their inordinate desire grows. A major theme of this book is that certain behaviors become addictive. Lustful activities certainly do.

Jesus knew the human heart. Once we give lust a place in our heart and mind, we want more—and more. We find a way to justify viewing sexually explicit images, and having justified it, we want more of it. Few stop at just one glance at a pornographic image. Continuing to view images leads to a search for a broader array of images—something that will stimulate in new ways.

As with other addictions, those viewing pornography find ways to normalize their behavior. "It's not hurting anyone" is a common refrain. Ask the wife of any man caught with a computer full of pornographic images if she has been hurt in the process. She'll firmly tell you yes. Why? Because she feels cheated on, objectified, and degraded. She feels as if he is not satisfied with her.

Pornography is often a gateway experience for greater degrees of deviance. As marijuana is a gateway drug for harder drugs, pornography often leads to increasingly sexually deviant experiences. It is critical to remember that sexual addiction is an addiction—it will lead to a desire for more and more experiences in order to gain the sought-after high.

The Affair

Conservative estimates are that 60 percent of men and 40 percent of women will have an affair at some time in their lives. Rarely do individuals have only one affair. One leads to another, and too frequently an affair becomes a part of marriage. With many opportunities for unfaithfulness, sexual addicts get their fix. They seek out conquests, multiple partners, in an endless effort to obtain their high. This inevitably leads to disappointment and pain.

If you've been the victim of an affair, you know the excruciating pain involved. Nothing is normal about cheating on your mate or being cheated on. This is why the Scriptures talk at length about sexual purity.

Kyle's wife, Kelly, speaks candidly about the impact of her husband's behavior.

"I can't understand it," she said tearfully. "I know he's been frustrated, but to cheat on me is disgusting. It's almost like he flaunts these women, knowing I'll catch him. Why am I not enough for him? He promises not to do it again, and then I catch him talking to some other woman, and it kills me. I think about leaving him but worry about our two little girls. And when I do threaten to leave, he promises to change. I don't get it."

What Kelly doesn't understand is that her husband's affairs are not really about her. Although his indiscretions are certainly personal and seem to have something to do with problems in their marriage, this doesn't justify his actions. Seeking relief from his pain, he acts out. Creating rituals has become reinforcing, ending in a pattern of behavior that will be hard to break. Kyle's sexually compulsive behavior is part of his addiction.

For many people, extramarital affairs are a sure sign of a sexual addiction. Forces within the individuals push them toward affairs, novelty, excitement, or new conquests. Feeling despair over their behavior, many seek comfort in another new relationship—and the cycle continues.

Adult Bookstores

Often located in a seedy part of town, adult bookstores are the epitome of sexual addiction. With neon lights and slimy posters in the windows, these stores appeal to base instincts. What could be so tantalizing inside? These stores have always had a negative connotation and probably always will.

Adult bookstores provide a place for people to act out their sexual addiction. Shrouded in secrecy and thus shame, these bookstores are magnets for "forbidden fruit." Every man I've counseled for sexual deviancy has frequented adult bookstores. Clearly, these men have been excited by the forbidden materials they find in these stores. Home to pornographic movies, books, magazines, and "toys," these stores have become part of the addictive cycle for many, an element in their ritual. These men look forward to the sexual experience they'll have at the store. With each adventure, their sexual addiction increases.

Sexual Fantasies

Sexual addictions begin in the brain. We're all looking for emotional and physical highs. Sexual addicts want the high as well and get it not only through particular behaviors but also from emotional hits gained from their sexual fantasies.

Long before a sexual addict goes to the adult bookstore or calls a woman for an encounter, he has fantasized about what is going to take place. He has rehearsed what took place the last time he engaged in this behavior. Sexual rehearsal is another way for addicts to get small emotional highs before the real encounter. Like a shopper who gets a high from a big afternoon shopping trip, sexual addicts have many experiences they can revisit again and again in their minds, igniting the serotonin transmitters.

We're all tempted to keep thinking about anything that gives us pleasure. Therefore, we should be cautious about what we allow ourselves to dwell on. If we allow ourselves to fantasize about sexual deviance and to continue viewing images that feed those fantasies that bring us pleasure, these thoughts become stronger in our minds.

We all have sexual fantasies. The key is what kind of fantasies we allow ourselves to have. Fantasizing about your mate in the context of a healthy, loving relationship is a great thing. Fantasizing about someone else's mate or about images you've viewed in a magazine will only lead to trouble.

The apostle Paul offers one of the strategies for managing our sexual thought life. He encourages us, "Be transformed by the renewing of your mind" (Romans 12:2). He contrasts believers with "those who have given themselves over to sensuality...with a continual lust for more," and he says, "be made new in the attitude of your mind" (Ephesians 4:19,23).

Criminal Behavior

Sexual impulses, left unchecked, may lead people to cross the line into criminal behavior. Sadly, the depths of sexual addiction can reach child molestation, indecent exposure, and predatory Internet behavior. Sexually criminal behavior has become a huge societal problem, taxing our resources for effective ways to deal with sexual addicts whose behavior has crossed legal lines.

Our society harshly judges those whose sexual behavior has violated others, and rightly so. Although these judgments are appropriate, we must again keep in mind that many of these individuals are addicted—they are not fully in control of their behavior. This can never, however, stop us from holding these individuals responsible for their actions.

Yet another aspect is worthy of our consideration. Almost without exception, these individuals have been victims of abuse themselves, thus giving credence to our understanding of generational abuse. Too often molesters have been sexually victimized themselves. Their own victimization doesn't excuse what they've done, but it helps us understand how one person can willfully harm another so egregiously.

Cross Addictions

We cannot talk about sexual addiction without talking about cross-addictions—the process whereby an individual is afflicted with more than one addiction. Sexual addicts are likely to be addicted to drugs, alcohol, or both. They might also be addicted to television and accumulation and be severely codependent. They may also have a co-occurring disorder, such as clinical depression.

Some hypothesize that when people give up one addiction, they're likely to develop another. Although little evidence supports this theory, much evidence supports the existence of cross addictions. When dealing with any particular addiction, clinicians should look closely for other hidden addictions as well.

Evidence also supports the premise of an addictive personality—someone predisposed to having addictive disorders. The verdict is still out, though quite clearly some people appear predisposed to struggle with many addictions. Giving up one may only be a start—they may need to overcome other addictions and take measures to heal from addictive aspects that influence their personality.

Breaking the Yoke of Bondage

Breaking the yoke of bondage to sexual addictions is difficult. Thankfully, many churches are recognizing the debilitating effects of this disorder and are offering instruction and support to help people break free from sexual addiction. Churches have taken a powerful step forward in treating sexual addicts by embracing 12-step programs such as Celebrate Recovery, which offers hope and healing for sexual addicts and their mates. Encouraged and empowered to speak openly about their problems, sex addicts are able to shed much of the shame that keeps the addiction secret and strong.

The first and most important step in dealing with any addiction is to admit your struggles to another person and to be accountable for altering your addictive cycle of behaviors. *Believing you can conquer sexual addiction alone is never appropriate.*

Support groups are critical places of healing, where others with the same problems gather to offer experience, strength, and hope. Sexual addicts are not second-class citizens—they are individuals who, because of unique aspects of their background, have succumbed to the powerful addiction of sexuality.

Breaking the bondage requires a specific plan of action. Patrick Carnes offers these steps, which have been found to be very helpful in breaking sexual addiction:

- *Make a sexual leap of faith.* Change is a gradual, not sudden process.

- *Sustain sex with intimacy.* Sexual vitality comes from relationships.

- *Talk before, during, and after.* Verbalizing passion, needs, and fears is perhaps the best way of facilitating sexual intimacy.

- *Overcome sexual shame through affirmation of each other.* Affirm the positive things you see and experience with your mate.

- *Respect boundaries and limits.* Building trust helps heal the sexual wounds of the past.

- *Pay attention to feelings.* Learn to label and express them.

- *See sex as a legitimate joy.* Abandon the rules you learned that kept you in addictive and co-addictive obsession. Have fun.

- *Take care of your body.* Physical health is basic to sexual health.[4]

Practicing these principles will set you on your way to overcoming sexual addiction.

The Sanctification of Sexuality

Society seems to say, "Do what you want and enjoy sex any way you want with whomever you want." But the Scriptures offer a better way—holding to respectful boundaries with pure minds and motives. We don't have to settle for a prudish, boring sexuality, nor do we have to succumb to an "anything goes" sexuality. We can find a way to recover from our wounded sexual past and live a liberated sexual future.

What does this look like? What does true sexual freedom mean? It means that we begin to embrace several truths:

First, sex was created by God for our delight. We don't need to shrink or hide from our enjoyment of sex. We don't have to be embarrassed by our pleasure in our mate.

Second, with God's help, our sexuality can be made new again. Jesus makes all things new (Revelations 21:5). Even if you've got a past of disappointment or degradation, you can start all over again with the power of God.

Third, sex is good. Everything created by God is good. We don't have to be ashamed of it. We can embrace its goodness. Sex, with the proper person, with respect and dignity, can be exciting.

Fourth, within the context of marriage, sex is sanctified. While many have made it ugly, in one respect or another, it can be a beautiful experience again.

Finally, we never have to be slaves to our desires. Our sexuality can be passionate but never needs to be idolized. Sex is for our enjoyment, but not to the exclusion of our relationship with God.

Thankfully, sexual addiction can be overcome. This requires courage and decisive action. It requires focus and, most importantly, the power of God in your life. You can experience freedom and learn to experience the joys of liberated sexuality once again.

Chapter Eight

Not Until Your Work Is Done!

If I were a medical man, I should prescribe a holiday to any
patient who considered his work important.

Bertrand Russell

"Drug addicts live on the streets and line up for their weekly methadone shots."

"Alcoholics can't make it through the day without drinking a half case of beer or a couple of rum and Cokes."

"Fat people are weak-willed and always seem to be eating a bag of potato chips."

Statements like these are made too frequently by misinformed people. We make these biased judgments without fully understanding the complexities of addictions. When we look at our own addictions up close, however, things are suddenly much different. Looking at my personal addictions has made the topic of addictions real—and I hope investigating yours has made the issue personal for you as well. Talking about the parade of addictions is easy in the abstract—as if they don't apply to you or me. But they do.

I've been able to write about addictions primarily in the abstract—until now. I don't struggle with alcoholism or drug addiction. I escaped the agonies of eating and sexual addiction. But work—now, that's something else. When it comes to work addiction, I'm hooked.

I previously mentioned that I am the son of a card-carrying workaholic. My father put in extremely long hours as a sales manager, came home for a quick bite of dinner, and then jetted out the door to distribute Bibles, practice in the church choir, or do bookwork related to his role as church elder. He was always busy.

His work was praised by others. He was promoted by his employer because of his industriousness. He was a strong leader, not only in our local church but also in denominational church politics. Everyone appreciated his leadership skills and his energy.

As the saying goes, "The apple doesn't fall far from the tree." My life has been replete with addictions to work and busyness, terms which I'll use interchangeably in this chapter.

Looking back, I can see that the roots of my addiction to busyness and work took hold in junior high. As an eighth grader, I had the biggest paper route in the city, and I bragged about my commercial success. I used my hard-earned dollars to purchase a Honda 50 motorbike that was the envy of all my buddies. I learned early that hard work had its rewards.

During high school, while many of my friends were playing, I chose to work extra shifts at Denny's and became addicted to busyness, work, and the things money could buy. I worked hard and enjoyed the "toys" I could afford, such as cars and stereos.

After I suffered a short lapse of industriousness in high school, my addiction picked up steam again in college and never let up until my emotional crash in 1990, when, as a result of sheer exhaustion, I began cutting back my work hours. Slowing down was not some virtuous decision on my part—my body was shot, my nerves were frayed, and my obstinate drive to succeed had collapsed.

Since that time I've been very interested in emotional, spiritual, and physical healing. I've parsed out my time and energy much more carefully in an effort to take better care of myself. One of my primary goals has been to live a balanced life.

Perhaps as you reflect on your life and the lives of those around you, you too will see a person who is out of balance. This problem is frequently compounded by the fact that our culture offers great rewards to those who refuse to rest.

Work Addiction

My father had reasons for working as hard as he did. He and my mother had five children; that makes seven mouths to feed. As products of the Great Depression, my parents were constantly beset by financial fears. My father worked long hours, and my mother worked as a schoolteacher. Both were industrious, wanting more for their family than they'd had as children.

But work has taken on a different meaning in our culture. Work has been part of our psyche since the garden, when Adam and Eve were told to tend the plants and animals. But we've gradually taken on more and more. This frame of mind sets the stage for work addiction and the chaos it wreaks in so many lives.

Workaholism is an addictive pattern similar to other process addictions and is intertwined with cultural and societal norms of working hard, achieving more, and reaching the American dream. Factories began operating around the clock as production demands increased. Everyone wants more, and we're tantalized into believing we can get it—if only we work a little harder. We take pride in how hard we work and often receive accolades from it. No other obsession in our parade of addictions is so well-rewarded by society as the compulsion to work.

My parents were not alone. Everyone seems to be pushing

harder and harder. My parents wanted two cars, a larger house, a summer cabin at the lake, and a boat to use on Puget Sound. Who could blame them? But what good are these things if you sacrifice your health, marriage, or family life, which often happens to those addicted to work?

How is it possible that we've transformed something so natural into an addiction?

Work addiction has been associated with the following behaviors:

- doing more than one thing at a time (multitasking)
- being impatient with interruptions
- feeling guilty if not working
- worrying about work
- committing to too many things
- focusing on outcomes rather than process
- continuing to work after coworkers are finished
- planning and thinking about future events and forgetting to live in the here and now
- establishing personal standards of perfection
- forgetting or ignoring important family celebrations and activities because of work
- not taking time to play

If you're like me, you see yourself in one or more of these symptoms. In our fast-paced culture, we can easily fall prey to multitasking, being impatient, and overcommitting. In fact, some of us feel guilty if we're *not* multitasking and overcommitting. Society expects us to move fast, work hard, and stay busy. And in the process, we'll be rewarded with materialistic gains.

Work addiction may initially seem out of place in this book, but it is similar to other addictions in that it comes with an adrenaline and dopamine high generated by staying later at the office and accomplishing more than the next person. As with other addictions, it can have serious consequences.

Extreme Workers

In today's economy, we've developed a new breed of workaholics. Technological advances enable us to be on the job at all hours of the day, in any situation. Sophisticated cell phones, including personal digital assistants, such as the BlackBerry—or "CrackBerry" as it's referred to in some circles—create a 24-hour work environment.

Our unhealthy work habits undoubtedly have their roots in our Puritan work ethic, which subscribes to hard work for the sake of hard work. But we've adapted and embellished on this ethic. In some circles we now refer to workaholics as *extreme workers.*

In recent years, with the dot-com phenomenon and the rise of such giants as Microsoft, Cisco, Google, General Motors, General Electric, and General Mills, companies began expecting more and more out of their employees. Teams of workers involved in cutting-edge advances are expected to work longer and longer hours. Overtime is expected, and in fact, 60- to 70-hour workweeks are glamorized. All the while, we rely on denial to tell ourselves that nothing is wrong with this.

In an article by Stephanie Armour for *USA Today* titled "Hi, I'm Joan, and I'm a workaholic," she says, "Workaholics have long been a part of the workforce. But new research shows a growing number of these extreme workers are driven to long hours on the job because of new technology, globalization and today's intensified business pressures."

Extreme workers typically put in 60 hours or more a week and exhibit characteristics such as unpredictable work flow, fast-paced work under tight deadlines, and incredible levels of responsibility that include managing other employees. They are also familiar with the profit and loss of the company and how the company fares in contrast to their competitors.

Armour also cited the following statistics:

- Sixty percent of high-earning individuals work more than 50 hours a week.
- Thirty-five percent work more than 60 hours.
- Ten percent work more than 80 hours.

Add a typical one-hour commute, and a 60-hour week means leaving home at seven a.m. and returning at nine p.m. five days a week.

Sylvia Ann Hewlett, president of the Center for Work-Life Policy, wrote in the *Harvard Business Review* that two-thirds of those defined as extreme workers don't get enough sleep, and half don't get enough exercise. Many also have problems with overeating, drinking, and anxiety. I'm guessing they also have trouble with maintaining healthy relationships and being effective parents.

Work addiction is quite similar to other addictions. It includes an excessive attachment to the activity, and compulsive actions are used to manage the anxiety associated with that activity. In other words, although work might be extremely enjoyable to extreme workers, at some point the tail starts wagging the dog, and the dog spins out of control.

Many extreme workers begin to lament their work schedules. Such was the case with a thirtysomething gentleman named John, whom I sat next to at Chicago O'Hare International Airport recently. He worked as an engineer at General Electric.

He fidgeted with his BlackBerry as we waited for our flight to Seattle, and I introduced myself. John was tall and slender and sported a crew cut. He was dressed in a gray business suit with a crisp white shirt and looked every bit the distinguished businessman. I admired his appearance as well as his state-of-the-art BlackBerry.

"Nice toy," I said, after watching him scroll through his messages for several minutes.

He smiled and said, "You mean the CrackBerry? Company-issued to make sure we're always within earshot. It really does save me a lot of time, and I couldn't get along without it. Real-time e-mail, conference calls, instant texting. Got to have it in the world of business."

"Sounds as though you really like it," I said.

"We all like 'em. And we all hate 'em. I suppose we like what they can do and how they've revolutionized business. It's just a matter of managing them and not letting them manage you."

"Sounds like the world of work for all of us," I said. "It all comes down to maintaining balance."

"I suppose that's true."

Curious about his business travel, I asked John to tell me more about his professional life.

"I travel at least 20 days a month," he said. "I'm never sure when I'll be home. I used to love the travel and the projects. Our technology is cutting-edge, and I can't think of a more exciting company to work for. But the job is a killer. I've been going at this pace for ten years and see no end in sight. We've got to stay ahead of the competition, or we'll lose market share—and we can't have that."

"I can't imagine traveling that much," I said. "The little bit I do takes a lot out of me."

"I do it because I do like the work. It's thrilling to be part of a team that is creating the newest technology in brain imagery, robotics, and cancer research. There's never a dull day."

"But I can tell by the way you're talking that there's a downside," I said.

"Well, I'm on my third marriage, if that tells you anything. And I never know which sport my son is playing because I can't keep track of him. I've never been to one of my daughter's piano recitals. Yes, there's a downside. No doubt about it. But if I scaled back, I know I'd miss the rush."

His words caught my attention. Clearly, a rush accompanies working on a team of creative people engaged in developing revolutionary concepts. John's job literally gave him an opportunity to change the world. When it comes to work addiction, he is not alone.

But I wondered if we have given enough thought to the cost of this high. Have we accurately labeled it as an addiction? Or do we grab our bag of excuses, rationalizations, and explanations, and whitewash the destruction that accompanies work addiction?

The Thrill, the Money

Many people are like John, flying around the country exhausted and working 60-plus hours a week for the thrill of it. They love the excitement and the money and unconsciously look for their next high, failing to truly count the cost.

Although I certainly have no interest in damaging my relationship with my wife or my children, I find something alluring about John's life.

Consider that John could quit his job and work nine to five for a manufacturing company. He could relinquish his BlackBerry, turn in his platinum airline card and his Hilton Honors Hotel card, and be home every night for dinner. But for a man accustomed to living on the cutting edge since his college days at Massachusetts Institute of Technology, this would be like a life sentence in Alcatraz. It's easy to understand why he struggles to let go of this lifestyle.

I've talked to a lot of business people during my travels around the country. I see the fire in their eyes as they turn on their phones the second the jet hits the tarmac. They're like an alcoholic who pours himself a drink the moment he walks into the house at night or the drug addict who starts thinking about her next high upon awakening in the early afternoon. Power, creativity, production, and money can be addictive.

Lest we think workaholism strikes only the sleek businessman, think again. I've seen the same fire in the eyes of a pastor intent upon building a bigger church. I recall being part of a growing congregation where the young pastor carried a BlackBerry, packed his days with meetings and appointments from morning to night, and prided himself on being available to his congregants at all hours. He wanted the latest, greatest, state-of-the-art audio-visual equipment for his sanctuary and ran his service like a Hollywood performance.

People became enamored with Pastor Steve's electrifying sermons, complete with PowerPoint images. They were caught up in a groundswell of emotion generated not only by the Spirit of God but also by the spirit of Pastor Steve. The sermon, music, colors, and lights were all used to orchestrate an experience, and Pastor Steve's status skyrocketed as a result. In the process, Pastor Steve was able to rationalize his behavior as being all for the glory of God.

However, I also noticed the price he paid, working 60 to 70 hours a week and neglecting his family, his marriage, and his health. Eventually, problems began to surface. People began sensing that church was more showbiz than worship—more the Pastor Steve Show than a gathering of believers and newcomers for fellowship, prayer, worship, and instruction in God's Word.

Becoming addicted to the pursuit of power, excitement, and money is easy. No one is immune from the temptation.

7-Eleven, 24/7

Our world has changed dramatically over the years. Now pastors have to ask people to turn off their cell phones prior to the start of the sermon. We're all connected—the lines between our personal lives and work have become blurred for many of us. But it wasn't always this way.

During the quiet 1950s, I recall walking a mile to a little corner store called Please U. My sisters and I gladly hiked that mile to buy penny candy with money from our allowances and from doing odd jobs for our parents and neighbors. We knew that little store was only open from nine to six and was closed on Sundays, and we timed our excursions accordingly.

I distinctly remember the opening of an unusual new store in our neighborhood in the early 1960s. People called it a *convenience store,* and it promoted its longer hours. Our agricultural society had previously followed a more traditional model. Work was reserved for sunup to sundown, with Sundays set aside for church and family.

Though always hard workers, my family took time to celebrate Sunday. It was a day reserved for church, dinner, friends, fellowship, and more church. We never thought about hitting the malls—there weren't any. We never thought about working more hours at the plant—it was closed. We never thought about running to any stores or squeezing a last drop of work out of our week. The day was reserved for worship and rest.

And then it happened.

The convenience store experimented with staying open from seven a.m. until eleven p.m. In 1962, 7-Eleven expanded to 24 hours. Now the largest chain store in any category, 7-Eleven has more stores than McDonald's.

The trend caught on. Other national chains began staying open later, and we began sliding into sacred territory—Sunday.

As a society, we're willing to stay open longer and be available anytime. Anything to be more productive. These are clear indicators of workaholism. We're willing to do nearly anything to lure a customer and make a sale.

Thanks, 7-Eleven!

We didn't need convenience stores, of course, to make us a society of work addicts. The stage had been set long before 7-Eleven began its experiment with longer hours and the advent of the 24-hour society. We have always been a country that worships work, productivity, and consumerism. We'd been creeping inexorably toward the seven-day workweek for years.

Although some decried the advent of shopping malls and 24-hour convenience stores, many celebrated these new opportunities. We could work harder and longer and make even more money. But when we opened our minds to this paradigm, we became prime territory for the development of work addiction.

Myths About Work Addiction

Grasping the severity of work addiction is difficult for us because work is so highly valued in our culture. Let's consider some of the common myths associated with work addiction:

- "You can't become addicted to work." This is not true. You can become addicted to this fast-paced life, driving yourself harder and harder. Many companies reinforce this addiction by pushing employees to produce more by tying employee wages, bonuses, and promotions directly to their productivity.

- "Work is not physically and psychologically addicting." Wrong. Work addicts achieve a high (from dopamine and serotonin) from making more money, striking a new deal, or beating their competitors. They invest a great deal in their work and find great psychological satisfaction from it.

- "Work addiction has no harmful effects." Not true. At some point, as was the case in my life, the wheels start to fall off the cart. You can't push yourself endlessly without physical, emotional, spiritual, and familial suffering.

- "We must all work this hard." This is one of the rationalizations we use for living more complicated lives. Although we may want some of the nice things we can purchase from working overtime, we don't have to labor as hard as many do. We can live with less and simplify our lives.

- "It's easy to quit working so hard." Work addiction, like other addictions, involves biochemical changes in our brain and complex sets of behaviors, so changing our lifestyles can be very difficult.

Work is healthy in many ways and is a natural part of our

society. Because work is good and necessary and comes with so many rewards, seeing it as something potentially destructive and even addictive can be challenging.

Affluenza

No discussion of workaholism would be complete without talking about a new disease in our culture, which has been called, quite appropriately, *affluenza*. According to the online encyclopedia Wikipedia, affluenza is a social theory that describes the negative symptoms arising from desiring to be materially wealthy.

Proponents of this theory suggest that those who experience affluenza find the economic success they've chased leaves them feeling unfulfilled, yet they wish for increased wealth. Individuals with affluenza often have significant wealth, placing a high value on money, possessions, appearance, and fame. But none of that brings them happiness.

Affluenza is particularly rampant in the United States, where we place a high priority on financial success and material possessions. We admire hard work so much that we promote those who are willing to sell their souls to the corporation.

Our media also reinforces material values through the adulation of celebrities and their way of life. We are teased by the high-gloss lifestyles of the rich and famous. We're told we can have it all. What we aren't told is the price we'll have to pay to get it and to keep it.

We are teased with images of large houses, fancy cars, and exotic travel, temptations that appeal to the part of us that feels unfulfilled. We push ourselves harder and harder, compelled to keep up with the Joneses regardless of the cost. We struggle with feelings that tell us we're not enough just as we are.

Of course, affluenza has crept into church, where the wealth and prosperity gospel flourishes. We are encouraged to plant seeds of faith, and abundance will be ours. We see television preachers' lavish lifestyles, and note that they see no inconsistency with this and Jesus' teachings.

Consumerism, as we've all discovered, offers little satisfaction. As proponents of the theory of affluenza suggest, chasing wealth and luxury leaves us feeling empty and depleted—just as other addictions do. We work harder to accumulate more, with material rewards offering a substitute for dopamine. We take pride in our gadgets, pleased by our ability to accumulate things. We may have previously said, "Look what I've done," but we now say, "Look what I've got."

Unfortunately, no luxury and no amount of money will make us feel complete. And for those afflicted with affluenza, no purchase will take away our incessant desire to purchase more. We keep pushing, and affluenza takes its toll on our bodies, minds, and souls.

Toward a Healthier Lifestyle

Immersed in our American culture, we can hardly imagine a different way of living. We are bombarded with glitzy advertisements on television and in magazines, so espousing a simpler lifestyle is like swimming upstream. To seek a remedy for affluenza is to move directly in opposition to our culture.

On a recent trip to Mexico, my wife, Christie, and I noted a far different mind-set among the non-Hispanics who live in the villages around Todos Santos, near the southern tip of the Baja Peninsula. At breakfast one morning, my wife and I had a conversation with Annie, an easygoing American woman in her forties, who shared the following story.

"I've been here for five years. Whenever I come back from visiting friends in California, it takes me several days to wind down. We don't run down here. When my friends ask what I do, I don't know how to respond. I tell them that I just live life. They seem frustrated with this response, as if I should be doing more. I moved here to escape the rat race, to stop accumulating things I don't need. I had to leave the U.S. to disconnect from the frantic pace that plagues most Americans."

I must admit that I don't fully understand her answer either. I quizzed her about exactly what she *did,* and I struggled to wrap my brain around a lifestyle not driven by the desire to accumulate more of something. I decided it was enough for me to see that there are other ways to live and that I can begin to consider them.

Understanding the problem is at least half of solving it. If we slow down enough to realize we're panting, barely able to catch our breath, we can take the next step and interrupt our destructive patterns.

Here are a few aspects of a healthier lifestyle that will help you gain some balance.

Stillness

At the other end of the spectrum from busyness, work, and accumulation are concepts completely foreign to most Americans—stillness, simplicity, and solitude.

Yes, I know you have children to get off to school, bills to pay, and dentist appointments to keep. I know about the desire to keep up with the Joneses. I'm familiar with the twisted pride I feel when my calendar is packed to overflowing.

The journey away from work addiction and toward healthy living begins with slowing down. You can enjoy stillness and reflection simply by reading and meditating on Scripture for a few minutes every day.

In her book *Invitation to Solitude and Silence,* Ruth Haley Barton tells how she arrived at the beginnings of stillness.

> Truth be told, it was desperation that first propelled me into solitude and silence. I wish I could say that it was for loftier reasons, pure desire for God or some such thing. But in the beginning it was desperation, plain and simple...In the midst of the outward busyness of my life there was an inner chaos that was far more disconcerting.[1]

Barton goes on to share details of her journey into stillness and explains how it revealed aspects of her emotional and spiritual life that needed attention. Over time, her body and soul began to respond to dedicated times of silence, so that eventually the very act of embracing this "set apart time and place" transported her to her own inner sanctuary.

I too have experienced personal retreats of stillness. At first, these were acts of desperation, designed to quiet the inner chaos I felt as a workaholic. I simply needed to calm my frayed nerves by putting a wall between myself and life's demands. Later, these quiet retreats were more deliberately chosen. They became times for reflection, prayer, and relationship with the Great Director who would help me sort out the spiritual challenges of my life.

Play

Play is an excellent way to mitigate the negative effects of a frenetic work life. But play, like stillness, is a foreign concept to the workaholic.

One of the barometers of a healthy work life is whether it is counterbalanced with a healthy play life. Sadly, many of us—myself included—have to remind ourselves to play. When we reach adulthood, something once so natural quickly becomes foreign if we take ourselves too seriously.

Shockingly, educators report that today's children don't know how to play. They are more driven, more competitive, more inclined to compete on video games than build forts and play on swings and monkey bars. Teachers now have to teach children something that should come naturally.

In 2004, the Alliance for Childhood, with the help of Olga Jarrett at Georgia State University, interviewed experienced kindergarten teachers in Atlanta. These teachers indicated that play had disappeared from their curriculum over the preceding ten years. They further reported that when they gave children time to play, the children didn't know what to do and had no ideas of their own. For those of us familiar with the creative minds of five-year-olds, this disturbing report bodes ill for the development of creative thinking.[2]

Unfortunately, the same is true of adults—when given time to play, we're not sure what to do. We're tempted to be productive, to make more money, and to do something worthwhile. We've forgotten that idle time and unstructured play can be time well spent.

True play has no goal except to play. There is nothing to achieve, no prizes for the fastest or best, no financial reward to the best player. People who play for the sheer joy of it enjoy experiences like these:

- walking on the beach
- skipping stones in the water
- picking wild flowers
- hiking
- sitting at an outdoor café with a cup of coffee and watching people
- swimming, running, and biking
- blowing bubbles
- laughing and telling stories

In an effort to combat the stress of our focused and busy lives, my wife and I routinely schedule a play date or field trip. We might attend First Friday in our hometown of Bainbridge Island, where we gather with artists to view their latest paintings, wood carvings, glass etchings, and other creative endeavors. We might take an automobile excursion around the island or a ferry trip to Seattle to have lunch with our kids.

Play might be walking the beach when the tide is out, kicking rocks and gathering beach glass. Play for us may involve a game of gin rummy without keeping score. When the days get longer and warmer, play will include sailing, that marvelous process of moving ever so slowly from one place to another and back again.

We are intentional about our play, aware of the temptation to fill all of our time with productive activities. We do what we can to keep our lives balanced by remaining alert to the dangers of excessive work and maintaining awareness that our work is enhanced when balanced with play.

What do you do for fun? How have you woven play into the fabric of your life? Has life become so crazy that you can hardly carve out time for fun? Are you like the kindergarten children who, when given a block of free time, weren't sure what to do with it?

Sabbath Rest

A study of the creation story reveals a majestic tempo and rhythm to life—a tempo that has been lost in our modern culture. Notice that God created (worked) for six days and then rested.

God didn't rest because He was tired. His rest, which He commanded us to undertake as well, involved creating a special place and time for self-renewal. God created the Sabbath so that we would not perversely work ourselves to death—which we seem so capable of doing.

We are instructed not only to cease our work but also to enter God's rest. What does that look like? Here is the prophet Isaiah's description:

> If you keep your feet from breaking the Sabbath and from doing as you please on my holy day, if you call the Sabbath a delight and the LORD's holy day honorable, and if you honor it by not going your own way and not doing as you please or speaking idle words, then you will find your joy in the LORD, and I will cause you to ride on the heights of the land and to feast on the inheritance of your father Jacob (Isaiah 58:13-14).

Keeping the Sabbath involves a lot more than not working. It involves more than not doing what we feel like doing. Isaiah suggests that it involves honoring and delighting in this holy day. Here are a few ideas for keeping the Sabbath holy:

- put work aside
- meet and worship with others
- delight in and celebrate our relationship with God
- serve and minister to others
- rest and rejuvenate

Work addiction is a debilitating process. I know. No longer in denial, I strive to maintain balance every day of my life. I am always on the lookout for times when my life is on the edge of spinning out of control. I routinely practice each of the balancing strategies listed in this chapter.

Whether you are a workaholic or you simply need to reexamine the pace of your life, consider making a few changes. Consider the possibility of adding a small dose of quiet and rest to offset your busyness. Add a splash of play and a dose of Sabbath rest to rejuvenate yourself. Choose to interrupt your work life long enough to balance it with other activities and create a space for God to make a difference in your life.

CHAPTER NINE

Chasing Your Losses

A faithful man will be richly blessed,
but one eager to get rich will not go unpunished.

PROVERBS 28:20

I'VE HEARD IT SAID that we can talk more easily about our sex lives than about our bank accounts. I think it's true. Many of us have an uneasy relationship with money, and those caught in the throes of addiction to gambling certainly live in this tension.

I'd never seen what gambling could do to an individual before I met Sam, a relatively new member of the fastest-growing group of addicts in America. An anxious 58-year-old who fidgeted as he sat in my office, Sam has a history of multiple addictions—alcohol first, which he says he has successfully kicked, and then drugs, which he has also left behind. But now he's deeply involved in gambling—both in casinos and on the Internet.

Sam entered my office with a vacant sadness in his eyes. He desperately wanted help with his gambling. Knowing little about this addiction, I searched my town for other professionals who might be of greater assistance but found no one. Even when I looked further in the larger town of Olympia, Washington, I turned up very few resources for gambling addicts.

Sam has not told his wife, Lindy, that we are meeting. He said if she knew the extent of his problem, his marriage would be over.

"No question about it," Sam said emphatically, his steel blue eyes meeting mine. "She'd divorce me quicker than anything. She barely hung on through my drug and alcohol problems. If she knew the amount of our retirement money I'm blowing at the casino, I'd be out on my ear. I've got to get things together, or I'm in deep trouble."

Sam appeared discouraged, his eyes hollow, his face grim, his full beard hiding the emptiness he feels about his life. He talked rapidly and anxiously about his need to find a solution to his gambling. Reluctantly, as if others might find out about his secret addiction, Sam shared his story.

"I was able to quit drinking," he announced proudly. "I just got to the point where booze wasn't doing anything for me anymore. I gave up marijuana without a problem too. But," he said, his voice trailing off, "I can't seem to give up the gambling."

"I'd like to know a little about the rituals you go through," I said.

Sam looked surprised and asked me what I meant. I explained Patrick Carnes' model of addiction, with cycles of preoccupation leading to rituals—special routines that lead up to the compulsive behavior. Finally, the addict is left with despair, feeling hopeless to control his behavior.

"That fits me pretty dang well," Sam said, tears welling up in his eyes. "I think I'm doing fine, and then I start wanting to chase the money I lost just a few days before. I go to the same casino, sit in the same section, order the same soda pop, play the same slots.

I keep track of how much I need to win back and how much I can afford to lose. I think somehow I'll be lucky this time, but it never works out that way."

Sam's life is out of control, and few resources are available for him. He believes others have more control of their impulses, that they work harder and move more directly and confidently toward retirement, which for him is very uncertain. Feeling like the odd man out, Sam wonders how he will overcome his gambling and Internet addictions.

Sam is like millions of other addicts—his life is sliding inexorably downhill, with all the hallmarks of addictive behavior. He searches compulsively for the high that comes from addictive behavior. He is unable to stop himself, despite the negative consequences. As a result, he experiences a troubling loss of control over his life.

Chasing Losses

Caught in a never-ending cycle of losses and lows, Sam struggles, and my heart goes out to him. He desperately wanted money to put back into his retirement account. Part of his work would require accepting the fact that his losses are just that—*his* losses.

Sam's challenges with gambling addiction came on the heels of drug and alcohol problems. He's racked up countless losses, and he is depressed. He wants not only to get his lost money back but also to create meaning in his life. He is tired of a life filled with wrestling addictions. Sam also wants to shake the pervasive feelings of guilt that came from knowing he threw away years of earnings and hard work, and he knows he still might face the wrath and rejection of his wife once she discovers what is going on with their finances.

When Sam isn't sneaking off to the casinos, he uses Internet technology to play the stock market and participate in interactive competitive games. He generally invests in high-risk stocks, often losing large sums of money. Here too he chases his losses, hoping for a big payoff that will bail him out. He imagines a jackpot that will repay his losses, satisfy his wife, and redeem him.

We can empathize with Sam. We too want to make things right with others we have wronged. We too are familiar with guilt and remorse, having made poor choices that affect others. Multiply these feelings many times over, and you will begin to understand gamblers' grief. Because their thinking is twisted, they will sneak off again and again to the slot machines in hopes of hitting the big one, the one that will take away all the sadness and loss.

Within this pursuit, we see Carnes' model—preoccupation, ritualization, compulsive behavior, despair. At some point, we want to grab addicts by the arm and yell, "Stop now! You can't win it back!" But of course, stopping is far easier said than done because their brains crave the high the addiction delivers. This is not a rational process. They are struggling with cravings, fears, hopes, and idealized dreams. They are listening to thoughts generated by a brain that is not functioning properly.

Dopamine Revisited

As we've discussed in this book, the addict's brain is not normal. We shouldn't be surprised to find that dopamine and serotonin are involved in the gambling addict's choices. The cravings of the brain drive his behavior.

Ronald Ruden, author of *The Craving Brain,* believes that compulsive behaviors—such as gambling, food binging, and alcoholism—are driven in part by the brain's pursuit of dopamine and serotonin.

> Addictive and compulsive activities are initiated by the same response: a rise of dopamine in the nucleus accumbens. For these behaviors, drinking alcohol (compulsive drug taking) to gambling (compulsive betting) reflect the brain's primitive biological response to try to biobalance itself. We are motivated to action.[1]

Many other studies have replicated Dr. Ruden's findings, supporting his contention that dopamine levels are higher in gambling addicts than in non-gamblers. The feelings of satis-faction generated by dopamine are so strong that one loses the ability to reason, thus leading to compulsive actions. The uncon-scious brain takes over, and logic goes out the window, leading to self-destructive behavior. People may actually believe that their behavior makes sense when in fact the craving for dopamine is driving their actions.

This is what is happening when people continue to gamble even though they know that the odds are unfavorable. In some cases, gamblers are brilliant and can determine the odds. Yet knowing that the odds are against them, they still bet. They somehow believe that the next pull of the slot may yield the huge payoff or the next hand of cards will bring instant wealth and success. The uncon-scious need for the release of dopamine becomes more important than rational acts of self-preservation and healthy functioning.

We must never lose track of our insights about the craving brain. We must resist saying or doing things that will shame the addict, and we must avoid offering quick remedies because they simply won't work. Although there is some measure of choice involved in these behaviors, we cannot use the word *choice* in the same way we would say that we choose where to park our cars. In the gambler's case, choice is compromised by the compulsive, craving brain.

Bells, Whistles, and Lights

I've never been captivated by drugs. I only drink alcohol in small quantities. But the bells, whistles, and lights, the *clang, clang, clang* of coins hitting the slot machine tray, and the people screaming "Jackpot!"—now that's a different story.

I understand why Sam and so many others swarm to casinos like bees to honey. Something about all those bells and whistles makes me salivate like Pavlov's dog. Something is contagious about hear-ing someone cry, "Jackpot!"

In my early twenties I was a sucker for Nevada road trips with my brother John and his wife, Joanne. On Friday night after work, we'd head out on a 12-hour trek to Reno. Anticipation ran high with thoughts of the big payoff spinning in my head.

An occasional smoker during those days, I found the noisy, smoky atmosphere of Harrah's to be tantalizing. Cheap drinks, the chance to hit the big one, and those cherries, oranges, and watermelons going round and round was hypnotic. Three oranges in a row meant twenty coins would hit the tray with a loud *ca-ching!* Even three cherries spit back five coins, keeping me in the game a bit longer. It's not hard for me to understand why people get lured back again and again for the chance to win big.

There was also a strong social aspect to the experience. In between pulls on the one-armed bandit, I'd carry on a conversation with John or Joanne or some stranger I'd just met. The conversations were always the same.

"Havin' any luck?" I'd ask the stranger, knowing I wouldn't get a straight answer. I sometimes kept track of how they were doing. If they had left their machine without winning, I'd wait until our conversation was finished and hop on, believing I had an increased chance of hitting a jackpot. I realize that this reasoning has no logic, but this is the way gamblers think.

"Things are a little slow today," they'd always answer whether it was the truth or not. No one wanted to reveal the exact nature of their fortunes, falsely believing they may be on a lucky machine, or have some edge over others.

I'd glance down at their bucket of money, assessing how much they'd made. I always had a wide range of feelings about other players who won—annoyance and envy but also hope that if they could win, so could I.

In the process, I'd make small talk with other gamblers. They all had a story and had traveled some distance, and they were generally friendly. This was a club—a select group of folks all hoping for the same thing—to win.

When the whirling wheel grew tiresome and my allotted money ran low, I'd head over to the keno lounge. I could slow things down while placing a bet that might bring me thousands of dollars. The walls were adorned with pictures of winners holding large checks, reminding us that someone really could win huge amounts of money. Rumors of big winners always floated around the lounge, but I never saw it happen.

My days of going to Nevada have come and gone. I gradually grew bored with the noise and clamor of casinos. No longer tempted by fast-pitch promises, I've moved forward with my life. But many can't and don't. I was fortunate not to get hooked.

Fastest-Growing Addiction

Most of us know about the drug epidemic in America. We're well aware of the dangers of alcohol and the untold lives affected by drunk drivers. Many of us have drug addiction and alcoholism in our genes and have been duly warned to walk carefully around these temptations.

Far fewer, however, are aware of the dangers of gambling and Internet addictions. Bernard Horn, in the book *Addiction: Opposing Viewpoints,* says, "Today, however, the fastest growing addiction in the U.S. is gambling. There are millions of adult pathological gamblers in America and, more ominous, millions of teenagers are addicted as well." Consistent with my premise that we are an addicted society, Horn adds, "Individuals are not alone in their addiction. State governments have become hooked on the revenues derived from casinos, slot machines, keno, and lotto. Thus, instead of warning citizens, many governments are exploiting them."[2]

The turn toward gambling in the U.S. is relatively recent since all states, with the exception of Nevada, prohibited gambling for years. Today, legalized gambling is everywhere—in all states except Utah and Hawaii. Forty-two states run their own lotteries, which in 2006 sold $52 billion worth of tickets. Many states encourage the establishment of Native American–run casinos or bingo halls, and 13 states allow commercial casinos (and tax them). There appears to be no limit to the growth of this industry. And it's all about the money!

Anne Wilson Schaef, in her book *When Society Becomes an Addict,* calls gambling one of the process addictions—where one becomes hooked on a process or a series of interactions or actions.

> The process becomes more important than the money. Like all addicts, compulsive gamblers use their addictions to keep them unaware of their internal feelings. Their lives become progressively more unmanageable. Gambling can be just as addictive as alcohol; although it does not destroy the body, as alcohol does, it is equally capable of destroying a life and of wreaking havoc with relationships.[3]

As Schaef is quick to point out, our culture supports and reinforces these addictions. No one shouts that the emperor is wearing no clothes. Casinos are growing at record rates, and state lotto programs have produced revenue windfalls. Poker has even become a nationally televised sport.

Destination Resorts

I am half amused and half disgusted as I pass a local mega-casino, replete with neon lights, valet parking, and covered walkways. Flush with profits, our casino owners are always in a building mode and continue to add multistory parking garages, luxury hotels, day spas, and buses that will pick up customers who don't want to drive. Clearly, there is money to be made, and casino operators are reaching out to a free-spending clientele. Casinos are becoming destination resorts and have mastered the science of *up-selling*.

It is no longer enough to entice the customer to come in and drop a few hundred dollars. These enormous resorts are now set on keeping you there for days, offering you lavish accommodations, sumptuous meals, and first-class entertainment. You'll be offered something special for your eyes, a relaxing experience for your body, and little reason to leave for days. Meanwhile, the gambling industry reels in millions of dollars, all in the name of entertainment.

I smile when I think of this because I am seeing an incredible sleight-of-hand. You're not being lured into a smoky backroom bar, where hucksters are out to lift your wallet and empty its contents. You're being treated to the time of your life, which will leave you feeling pampered, surprised, delighted, and entertained at the highest level. You'll even get to gamble along the way, and you'll be promised access to "the most generous slots in the state."

Ever so subtly we're being escorted toward a new paradigm. State-sponsored and state-promoted gambling has contributed to a societal acceptance of gambling as a natural part of our culture. New forms of gambling arise daily. Gambling is not seen as a nasty vice but as a promising shot at riches, entertainment, and glamour.

One client of mine, Cherie, excitedly tells of going to a casino in Newport, Oregon, where she and her girlfriend stay in a luxury hotel and spend the weekend. She and her girlfriend have gone dozens of times, and she clearly loves the experience. She says she is treating herself to a weekend away. Shopping, fine meals, wonderful entertainment—what's not to like about it?

Cherie isn't embarrassed to tell me about this excursion. In fact, she frames the experience as therapeutic—a relaxing weekend away from the rat race. She feels no shame, and her eyes light up in anticipation of her time at the beach. I nod and smile with some understanding. Casinos have become part of our social framework.

Cherie is not addicted to gambling, so her experience will be different from Sam's. She is not chasing lost money, and she is not hiding her gambling. She knows the odds are against her, even if she does exaggerate her possibility of winning. She doesn't emphasize it because the casino has succeeded in making sure that customers don't view losses as the central focus of the experience. She is buying an experience, and as long as the resort can deliver, everyone is happy.

My client is a new breed. She doesn't go to win, though doing so is always nice. She wants good food, lively entertainment, beautiful accommodations, and a chance to forget about her loneliness and impending divorce. She succeeds on all fronts, though the day may come when she is not able to choose as easily as she can today.

For now, Cherie can wrap her experience in the language of "a weekend away with the girls." Harmless, entertaining, and loads of fun. Others, however, are not having as much fun. They're losing their lives.

Corrupted Logic

Sam has taught me a thing or two about gambling addictions. Many forms of "addictive thinking" combine to shape the addict's thought process. The logic of the gambler is often significantly corrupted. Lance Dodes, author of *The Heart of Addiction*, explains:

> Making use of the new way of thinking about addictions, a reason for the emphasis on luck immediately jumps out. Since it is critical in addictions to reassert control against helplessness, it follows that anything that will aid this sense of control will be eagerly sought. A major problem with gambling, after all, is that by its very nature it cannot be accurately predicted.[4]

When listening to Sam and other gambling addicts, I hear corrupted logic. I hear patterns of behavior and thinking that create powerful rituals for individuals. As I listen to Sam, I hear various forms of magical, addictive thinking:

Superstition. Gambling addicts are commonly superstitious: They refer to lucky tables, lucky decks, and even lucky numbers. Many gamblers even believe they can predict which tables will be hot, and which won't. They believe in their own hunches and are sure they'll work—even when they don't!

The hot-hand. This fallacy is committed every day in casinos around the world whenever a gambler thinks he's hot. When gamblers are on winning streaks and keep betting or increasing their wagers to take advantage of their good luck, they fall victim to this type of thinking. Their fundamental mistake is the failure to appreciate statistical independence. Just as a fair gambling device does not remember its past, it also does not remember a gambler's past. A gambler's odds of winning a bet are in no way affected by whether the gambler has won or lost previously.

Intellectual mastery. Many gamblers work to improve their odds against the system and believe they have figured out ways of improving their odds. For example, people who bet on sports events carefully study information about the teams. Although this may seem reasonable, the odds are determined by collective wisdom, and so there really is no way to beat the odds.

A system for winning. This is simply a variation on the point made above. Gamblers believe that if they study the roulette wheel, count cards long enough, or read enough books about poker or blackjack, they'll be sure to win. Although this contains the tiniest element of truth, you can be sure that if there were a surefire way of winning, the casinos would know about it before you.

The next bet. Gamblers are often driven by the belief that the next bet is the answer to all their problems. The gambler has narrowed his thinking to the ridiculous point that this one win, in this one moment in time, can wipe away his sins of the past and make him feel wonderful. And theoretically, it could—for the briefest moment of time, until the cycle was started all over again. One bet cannot possibly end all of his problems.

Gambler's fallacy. Gambler's fallacy is the belief that an event that has not happened is due to occur. It is also called "the maturity of chances." Gamblers falsely believe that each play is *not* independent of previous plays and that their luck is sure to change. But luck doesn't change, and generally odds stay the same with each roll of the dice or pull of the machine arm.

Of course, these themes have many variations. Each of these illusions is based on the drive within to win—to get something for nothing. Then, after gamblers are hooked and broke, they want to win back what they've lost. In the end, however, they are left feeling defeated and depressed.

Internet Gambling and Addiction

Addictions blur the lines, and many people struggle with multiple addictions. Internet gaming addictions are cousins to other gambling addictions, feeding the same desire and thrill to win or to compete against others for money or prizes. Many individuals are at the mercy of more than one addictive process, and they are in denial about the harmful effects.

Many of those addicted to gambling also turn to the Internet, seeking the thrills and excitement that come from gaming, video viewing, and an assortment of other possibilities. The Internet has become an unrestricted opportunity not only to compete with others online and wage bets but also to show off in almost any way imaginable—all in the protected safety and anonymity of your home.

With the advent of the Internet came new ways to gamble, to pit our intellectual skills against those of others who are online. It is impossible to mention all of the possibilities for Internet gaming addictions. What follows are a few of the possibilities:

- *Video games.* Many individuals' addiction playing computer video games hampers their family and social relationships or disrupts their school or work life. As with other addicts, these individuals are often caught in a web of denial about the danger and damage this addiction is causing.

- *Interactive gaming.* Many find an alternate society on the

Internet. Through interactive gaming, they meet friends and connect with a social network to which they can belong. Of course, these networks often remove these individuals from the real world, and the games can be extremely addictive.

- *Internet surfing.* Many computer addicts spend hours surfing the Internet. They log on to favorite websites and meet friends in chat rooms or on social networking sites such as MySpace and Facebook. They feel as though they *must* check in as a routine part of their day.

- *Chat rooms.* Chat rooms have become "third places" in our society, after work and family, where we greet and meet our friends. These virtual gathering places have become very powerful and important places to connect with others.

- *Computer gambling.* Many use their computers to bet on sporting events or play cards or casino-style games in real time with other players. Individuals can also get real-time information with which to place more sophisticated bets.

- *Cell phone use.* Cell phones are becoming more sophisticated, blurring the line between phone and computer. With more cell phones having e-mail, text, and Internet capabilities, the temptation for greater and greater use exists. As with other addictions, excessive cell phone use seems to be increasing.

- *Blogging.* What better way to find out what people think than to follow their blogs? You cannot only discover what they think but also join in and become part of a virtual society in which people share their thoughts.

- *Internet addiction disorder.* This term describes the behavior of those who use the Internet excessively. People struggling with Internet addiction disorder report a compelling need to devote significant amounts of time to checking e-mail, talking in chat rooms, or simply surfing the Net, even though these activities cause them to neglect work, family, or other important obligations.

What are some danger signs of Internet use? Here are a few signals to watch out for:

- not keeping up with schoolwork, or work obligations
- lying about computer or video game use
- playing video games or using the Internet to the point that family, social, or work obligations are neglected
- dropping out of other social groups
- obsessing about being on the computer
- exhibiting increased irritability, anger, or even depression
- living an online fantasy life that replaces real-life relationships with family and mate

The Internet is an exciting, useful technology with an immense potential for education, entertainment, and addiction. Although we tout the incredible possibilities that the Internet delivers (and there are many), we must also admit that it provides a temptation for excessive use, including craving or compulsive use, loss of control, and continued use in spite of negative consequences—all the elements of an addiction. With untold possibilities for entertainment and excitement (euphoria) as well as social reinforcement, the stage is set for addiction.

Societal Impact

When we wire our homes for high-speed Internet and purchase the latest personal digital assistants and cell phones, we are toying with something that is highly addictive. With something so titillating offering portals to exciting images and experiences, can we manage our impulses to set healthy limits on our Internet use?

Computer use has reached well beyond work and functionality to the point that it now overlaps with fun and entertainment. Although we appreciate the capability of the Internet to provide us with sought-after solutions, more often we're surfing the Net out of boredom or to excite our senses. Other people are doing the same, so no social stigma is attached to this addiction. As with casinos and gambling, the Internet offers excitement at the stroke of a key. Very few venues can match it for accessibility and stimulation.

We're moving rapidly into an age where nearly every room will have high-definition televisions and high-speed Internet access. Couples are together, yet they are interrupted consistently by the ringing of their cell phones. Many feel estranged from one another, as each are engaged in their solitary, isolated worlds.

Recently, my wife and I attended a wedding and were only mildly surprised when, just before beginning the ceremony, the pastor asked the congregation to turn off all cell phones. The need to regulate such rude behavior suggests the consequences of living in our mobile, always-connected world.

Driven to Distraction

With each passing generation we seem to lose the ability to be with ourselves. We want to be on the go, frenetic with action, our heart pounding, our emotions vibrating, and our feet moving.

Perhaps more than anything, addictions take us away from ourselves. We can't possibly have a healthy relationship with ourselves when we're attached to an addictive process or substance.

I've encouraged Sam to journal—partly because I hope it might interrupt his compulsions and also because I want him to create a relationship with himself. I've seen the power of journaling in my life and believe it can help others. I want him to take a few moments every day to note how he feels, what he thinks, and what he wants.

I also want Sam to become more familiar with the work of God in his life. The Scriptures tell us, "Be still, and know that I am God" (Psalm 46:10). Our relationship with God is enhanced by solitude. Sam believes in God and wants to grow in that relationship. He can't do it, however, if his brain is craving a trip to the casino.

Sam is desperately estranged from himself and God, ritually focused on the high-tech gadgetry he uses to surf the Internet and on the spinning wheels at the local casino, where he plays slots. Each activity takes him further from himself and anesthetizes him to the anguish resulting from his addiction.

Mesmerized by the slot machines, Sam is driven by external stimuli. Scanning his PDA, Sam is temporarily transported to a nicer place. After all, Sam doesn't like his life, he doesn't like himself, he feels estranged from God, and he keeps myriad secrets from his wife, which increases their distance from one another. A little dopamine offers temporary relief.

Sam appreciates the opportunity to talk to me about his problems. He wants a fuller life, a richer life that isn't dictated by the casino, the Internet, and money. In many ways though, he's very bored. Sam wants a life with fewer ups and downs. He doesn't want to rue the stock market's down days or constantly worry about blowing another $500 at the casino.

Sam wants a normal life, as do any addicts. He wants friends and enhanced relationships with his wife, three children, and two grandchildren. He wants to begin planning for a happy retirement. He comes to therapy aware of the changes he needs to make to become a healthier, happier, and freer individual.

New Relationship with God

Besides taking us away from ourselves, addictions take us away from God. Every hour we spend sitting in front of the computer screen or gazing mindlessly at the slot machine or even texting friends is time we are not spending with God.

Gambling and Internet addictions take us away from the real

world, and an important part of that real world is our relationship with God. Breaking the bonds of addictions, therefore, must include a conscious decision to increase our contact with God—we must be deliberate about making time for God in our lives.

Jesus had a lot to say about money and distractions. One of my favorite passages concerns our priorities. "Do not store up for yourselves treasures on earth, where moth and rust destroy, and where thieves break in and steal. But store up for yourselves treasures in heaven, where moth and rust do not destroy, and where thieves do not break in and steal" (Matthew 6:19-20).

This is such practical counsel. Ask Sam how the lure of the jackpot has altered his life. Walk with him a short time as he chases after the dollars he's lost, and you'll see a desperate man. But listen closely and you'll find that he still hopes to end his addiction. He is tired of chasing after riches and excitement. He wants to renew his contact with God.

Jesus knows the folly of chasing after riches. He knows that these pursuits are ultimately dehumanizing. "For where your treasure is, there your heart will be also," He said (Matthew 6:21).

If we foolishly seek riches, we will treasure them and be sorely disappointed—if not addicted. But if we pursue our relationship with God, we will have invested wisely.

CHAPTER TEN

When Pleasing Others Is Hurting You

*The "give and take" that we all accept as an integral part of
life and love is actually pretty complicated.*

IRWIN KULA

WHILE WALKING ON THE BEACH RECENTLY, my wife and I approached a large flock of birds. As we neared the group, the pelicans and gulls scattered, leaving one bird behind. The lone, frightened gull hobbled away from us, unable to fly.

I pointed out the wounded gull to Christie, and we let out a sigh in unison.

"It's hurt," I said.

"Yes," Christie answered. "The poor thing."

"We've got to do something."

"Like what?" Christie said.

"I want to take it home."

"And then what?"

"We'll find a way to fix it."

"We all want to lend a hand, David, but it isn't always that simple."

"But what will happen to the bird?"

"I don't know," Christie said, her voice trailing off.

As we resumed our walk, I glanced back at the wounded bird. I couldn't help thinking that nature would soon take its course, as it does with all living things.

My desire to fix the bird came from the same place in me that wants to repair everyone's emotional damage. I want to wave a magic wand and make the pain go away. I want peace and joy. I want harmony. I want love.

But is my desire to fix things always a good one? I sometimes wonder.

It is good and useful when I help others while keeping my involvement within healthy boundaries. It is less than helpful when I work too hard to fix others who need to take more responsibility for finding their own way. It is not useful when my motivation is to please others or to make an impression.

Fixing others by living outside our abilities and responsibilities is an example of the last addiction we'll discuss in this book—codependency, or approval addiction.

We've discussed the challenges of the alcoholic, drug addict, sexual addict, gambling addict, food addict, and work addict. Now I want to expand our understanding of addictions by talking about people rarely considered to be an addict—approval addicts. Like me, they want to fix and control others. Like me, they seek approval from others. In some ways, they demand the approval of others.

How can someone so ostensibly nice, so outwardly pleasant, so seemingly sweet as the codependent ever be considered an addict?

As you will recall, an addict is anyone whose life is controlled by something or someone other than themselves. Addictions involve a substance or process that is used repeatedly in spite of its debilitating effects. The addiction process continues because of denial. Codependency meets these same criteria.

Approval addicts are controlled by others' opinions of them. They are controlled by trying to make others accept them, approve of them, and do what they want them to do. In so many respects, their lives are dictated by others.

Addictions and Codependency

Codependency was first identified by early addiction specialists, who discovered that those intimately involved with an addict were likely to display certain debilitating traits. In fact, the partner of an addict was identified as a co-addict, or codependent.

It certainly makes sense that people living with raging alcoholics would develop coping strategies to help them avoid invoking the anger of the alcoholics. Early researchers discovered that codependents tiptoe around addicts. Even more disturbingly, codependents often incorporate many of the addicts' thinking errors. While complaining about the problems stemming from their relationship with the addicts, codependents also enabled the destructive relationship to continue, losing their individuality in the process.

This enmeshed, dysfunctional relationship, in which at least one person is an addict or is emotionally unhealthy, becomes the breeding ground for codependency. Whether in a marriage, friendship, or family relationship, one unhealthy person has the capacity to spoil the whole bunch.

Later researchers and authors such as John Bradshaw, Sharon Wegscheider-Cruse, Robert Subby, and Pia Mellody expanded the earlier definition of codependency to include many more people, including myself. Just when I thought I could slip away from our parade of addicts by admitting to only one addiction, I realized I had to face my approval addiction. As surely as I had to admit to being a work addict, I also had to admit to struggling with codependency.

This topic can be quite confusing. How can I sometimes be a self-centered chump but at other times put myself on the line to help others? How can I be so other-oriented, while simultaneously depriving those I love of my energy and attention?

Millions of us would walk ten miles out of our way, barefoot, to avoid conflict with others, selfishly ignoring the impact of such behavior on our family and friends. We tell ourselves that we dare not hurt others' feelings, but at the same time, we are neglecting the needs and feelings of our mate and our children. This is confusing and apparently contradictory. And it's called codependency!

Melodie Beattie popularized the phenomenon of codependence with her bestseller *Codependent No More.* The subtitle of the book offers a hint at the apparent contradiction that accompanies codependence: *How to Stop Controlling Others and Start Caring for Yourself.*

Beattie admits that definitions about codependence are fuzzy and confusing. Originally, the term *codependent* was applied to one who had a relationship with a dysfunctional person, such as an alcoholic. But that definition has been broadened substantially. Beattie says, "A codependent person is one who has let another person's behavior affect him or her, and who is obsessed with controlling that person's behavior."[1]

This other person might be someone with significant problems we are trying to fix or a controlling person whom we are trying not to upset. The emphasis is on *our* behavior—we are trying not to rock the boat, or we're trying to make someone do something they'd rather not do. With all this focus on the other person, we get lost in the shuffle.

We must be careful, however, to remember that the codependent can also be controlling. We often want things to go our way. We may appear completely passive, but often beneath this calm exterior we may really want to exert control ourselves.

Here's another way to understand this phenomenon. A codependent person reinforces a weakness in someone else by ignoring it.

This happens when we tiptoe around the rage-aholic, hoping he won't lose his temper around us. It happens when we decide not to bring up a touchy topic because we don't want to make someone angry. This can also happen in a family or group when we don't speak openly about a problem because we don't want to be seen as troublemakers or don't want to risk rejection.

The key is to determine whether you have given up part of your identity by trying to please others. If that is the case, it is time to embark on a journey of recovery.

Symptoms of Approval Addiction

Pia Mellody, in her book *Facing Love Addiction,* helps us understand the complex nature of the codependent. She says codependents have problems with immaturity, often stemming from early family problems.

Consistent with findings by Melody Beattie, Pia Mellody found that codependents have the following symptoms:

- Difficulty experiencing appropriate levels of self-esteem. They are easily influenced by others and struggle to love themselves.
- Difficulty setting functional boundaries with other people. They allow others to violate their emotional (and perhaps even physical) boundaries, leaving them feeling vulnerable and unprotected.
- Difficulty owning their own reality. Susceptible to others' perceptions, they struggle to know what they think and feel and to share that appropriately.
- Difficulty addressing their adult needs and wants. They struggle with knowing how to effectively care for themselves.
- Difficulty experiencing and expressing their reality in moderation.[2]

Mellody also listed several behavioral traits that create problems for the codependent. She noted that recovery from codependence must address the following issues:

- *Negative control.* Codependents may try to control others by telling them who they ought to be, thus creating a sense of comfort for the codependent. On the other hand, they may allow others to control them because they desire to keep others comfortable.

- *Resentment.* Codependents tend to be angry people and feel resentful about being victimized. When people feel victimized, they often experience a loss of self-esteem and a profound need to stop the victimization. The resentment they feel, however, doesn't stop the victimization process.

- *Impaired spirituality.* Codependents either make someone else their higher power through hate, fear, or worship, or they attempt to become someone else's higher power.

- *Addictions or mental or physical illness.* Our ability to face reality is directly related to our ability to develop a healthy relationship with ourselves. This requires loving the self, identifying the self, caring for the self, and moderating the self.

- *Difficulty with intimacy.* Intimacy involves sharing our own reality and receiving the reality of others without either party judging that reality or trying to change it.[3]

Rachel came to see me for counseling, primarily because of problems with depression. Fifty years old and morbidly obese, Rachel had *victim* written all over her. She voiced her discouragement and feelings of depression. However, beneath her soft-spoken, passive demeanor, Rachel seethed with resentment.

Rachel told me she had been in counseling many times in the

past but had not found relief from her depression. In exploring her depression, she shared that she's been married to a chronic alcoholic, Mike, for 30 years. Their marriage has been a major disappointment to Rachel, but she indicated that she has come to accept his drinking problem.

"There's not much I can do about it," she said sullenly. "He's going to drink whether I nag him or not. In fact, the angrier I get, the more he drinks. So I do my thing, and he does his."

I asked her to describe the history of their marriage.

"We used to be so in love," Rachel said with a half-smile. "He didn't drink so much in the early years. We have two kids, and they're doing pretty well, in spite of being raised in a home with an alcoholic father. We have two grandkids, and they're the joy of my life."

"How do you and your husband relate?" I asked.

"He disgusts me most of the time. I've distanced myself from him, and he doesn't like that. But it's the only way I know to cope with his drinking. I've hollered and screamed, but he won't get help. He refuses to come to counseling."

"You're understandably angry."

"I'm not sure how angry I am," she said defensively. "I've pretty much accepted his drinking, but I feel like I've wasted so many years trying to get him to change, and it's all been for nothing. I'm stuck with him, and he's ruined my life."

"I understand your feelings," I continued, "but I'm wondering what you've done to take care of yourself. What have you done to improve your life?"

"What can I do, living with a hopeless alcoholic?" she asked with irritation. "I cope. That's about it."

As I began working with Rachel, I considered Mellody's list of processes that cause codependence.

Understandably, Rachel had been caught up in trying to control her husband. She had tried to change him, but she had also allowed him to victimize her. Rachel said that Mike had an anger problem and that she often tiptoed around him to ensure that he wouldn't become angry with her. She limited her activities because of his control. Her world had become painfully small.

There was no question about Rachel's resentment. Though she tried to minimize it, her resentment poured out of her at the mention of the word *alcohol*. She'd obviously been furious at Mike for the years she felt were wasted in a loveless marriage. She resented the control he had over her life and hated tiptoeing around him. She blamed him for all of her problems.

Rachel also experienced impaired spirituality. Although she was a Christian and attended church regularly, she angrily wondered why God had not cured her husband's alcoholism. She felt resentful about having to stay in a marriage that failed to meet her needs. Ironically, she had also made her husband a god by focusing so much of her energy on trying to change him.

Rachel also had a related food addiction—she relied on eating to comfort her in times of distress. She wondered during her counseling sessions if she was using food and her weight to deliberately create distance between herself and her husband. She made it clear that she didn't want a physical relationship with him and wondered if her weight gain was a way to make certain they had no sexual life.

Finally, Rachel had difficulty with intimacy. She had long since stopped trying to share her thoughts and feelings with Mike, and he no longer shared his thoughts and feelings with her. Their marriage was a marriage of convenience and duty. Nothing more. Neither wanted a divorce, but there was little love between them.

I felt bad for Rachel. Her problems were anything but simple, and I could understand why she was so discouraged. Mike had no intention of quitting drinking or entering recovery, and he was unwilling to go to counseling in an effort to save their marriage. Any changes would have to be initiated by Rachel. In the meantime, there were no simple answers for finding her way back to a healthy sense of self-esteem or a healthy marriage. She faced significant problems, layered one on top of the other, and becoming healthy again would take a great deal of work.

If Rachel simply settles, she will remain lost and discouraged. She must come to fully understand her codependency, realize how she enables a destructive process to continue, explore options, and be willing to take decisive action.

Codependency Trap

You can see how codependency can be a trap that ensnares and suffocates. You can get lost trying to follow the rules by living up to everyone's expectations but your own.

Barry Weinhold, Janae Weinhold, and John Bradshaw, in their book *Breaking Free of the Co-dependency Trap,* say codependency is a problem that is so stifling that it inhibits one from becoming a fully functioning adult. Living for so long with no goal other than to please others, codependents lose sight of who they are and what they believe. Bradshaw and the Weinholds provide the following list of traits of a codependent person:

- being unable to distinguish your own thoughts and feelings from those of others
- thinking for others and feeling responsible for them
- seeking the attention and approval of others in order to feel good
- doing things to please others when you really don't want to
- believing others know what is best for you better than you do
- focusing on others and their happiness
- whining or pouting to get what you want
- feeling unappreciated
- being afraid of making mistakes

- failing to express your opinion for fear of rejection
- pretending things are not as bad as they are
- feeling powerless to change your situation[4]

We can see Rachel in many of the symptoms listed above. Perhaps you can identify your own traits of codependency. Although anyone may possess one or two of the traits, if several are evident in your life, you probably struggle with codependency.

All of us display some symptoms of codependence at one time or another. If we are emotionally healthy, however, we don't lean exclusively on others for our sense of well-being. We don't try to control their behavior, nor do we allow them to control ours. We don't need approval from others in order to feel secure about our choices.

Approval Addiction

Beneath Rachel's dysfunctional relationship with her alcoholic husband was a tremendously insecure woman. Although she was 50 years old, in many ways she seemed quite childish. She came across as whiny and helpless and suffered from extremely low self-esteem. She blamed all of her problems on her husband, and she took little responsibility for choices she would need to make to become healthy.

This is part and parcel of the problem. By desperately seeking acceptance from another or in attempting to control the behavior of another, we lose confidence. In trying to gain another's approval, which may not be forthcoming, we lose our sense of security and often become trapped in a vicious circle. Joyce Meyer describes this in her book *Approval Addiction:*

> There is an epidemic of insecurity in our society today. Many people are insecure and feel bad about themselves, which steals their joy and causes major problems in all their relationships...Those who have been hurt badly through abuse or severe rejection, as I have, often seek the

approval of others to try to overcome their feelings and use the addiction of approval to try to remove the pain.[5]

Meyer tells us that seeking the approval of others is an addiction when the process becomes compulsive—people feel that they cannot do without approval and must have it to eliminate the inner pain they feel.

Addictions, you remember, are often attempts at finding relief, and this is certainly the case with approval addiction. Addictions involve the craving brain seeking dopamine or serotonin, or sometimes simply seeking relief from suffering, which seems the case with the approval addict.

Approval addicts are, in the words of Meyer, "people pleasers." She says that approval addicts "need approval so desperately that they allow themselves to be controlled, manipulated, and used by others. They are not led by the Holy Spirit, as Scripture instructs us to be. People pleasers are fear-based individuals."[6]

Approval addiction leads to bondage. Although it doesn't include the craving of a substance, it is a craving for approval. This compulsive craving for acceptance, appreciation, and admiration costs us our individuality and freedom.

Christian Giving

"But aren't we supposed to lose our lives in service of others?" some might ask.

This is the first criticism I received in response to my book *When Pleasing Others Is Hurting You*. Some Christians were immediately defensive, asserting that we're called to give up our lives, to die to ourselves daily. Some went so far as to say that there is no limit as to what we should do to please others. We are called to serve, serve, serve, some said.

Is that true, or is that a recipe for bondage and addiction? Can we serve others out of a healthy sense of self instead of being addicted to approval?

The Scriptures sometimes appear contradictory when it comes to serving others. Without close scrutiny, the Christian faith may appear to be marked exclusively by service. Christianity may seem to lead to death to the self and a singular focus on the needs of others. The apostle Paul says, "Each of us should please his neighbor for his good, to build him up" (Romans 15:2). Paul also indicated that he tried to please men so that they may be saved (1 Corinthians 10:33).

Although Paul tried to please men, he ultimately asserted the importance of only pleasing God. He was not afraid of displeasing men and did not seek to be popular with others. He wanted to fulfill God's calling on his life.

The critical issue concerns motives. Why are we doing what we're doing? If we're assisting in children's church because we feel gifted in that area and sense God's call in that arena, we will feel blessed and be a blessing to others. If, however, we perform these actions out of guilt and to seek approval, we'll soon burn out from exhaustion and resentment.

If we tolerate hurtful words, turning the other cheek because we truly sense it is better to let an issue slide, we will experience peace by doing so. If, on the other hand, we don't set a boundary on an abusive action out of fear of disapproval, we'll soon feel resentment, leading to a broken relationship. Motive is everything.

Many Christians struggle with the issue of being nice. They live by a set of rules inconsistent with Scripture, such as these:

- Always be nice.
- Never disagree with anyone.
- Never cause conflict.
- Always give.
- Always serve others.

Many Christians work overtime at being nice. They perform acts of service out of obligation, not out of desire or choice. Motivated by fear, they say yes when they really want to say no. Subsequently, they burn out and become resentful, experiencing very little delight.

Paul encourages us to "speak the truth in love" (Ephesians 4:15). We will sometimes feel called to talk out a conflict with a brother or sister, sharing our feelings honestly (see Matthew 18:15-17). This is consistent with Scripture.

Loss of Self

As with each of our addictions, the result of our codependency is ultimately a loss of relationship to ourselves. As codependents, we're so focused on others that we lose sight of who we are and what we believe.

In the poignant opening to her book *The Heart of a Woman,* Maya Angelou tells of her struggle to find herself and be herself.

> I had returned to California from a year-long European tour as premier dancer with *Porgy and Bess.* I worked months singing in West Coast and Hawaiian night clubs and saved my money. I took my young son, Guy, and joined the beatnik brigade. To my mother's dismay, and Guy's great pleasure, we moved across the Golden Gate Bridge and into a houseboat commune in Sausalito where I went barefoot, wore jeans, and both of us wore rough-dried clothes…. During our stay in Sausalito, my mother struggled with her maternal instincts. On her monthly visits, dressed in stone marten furs, diamonds and spike heels, which constantly caught between loose floorboards, she forced smiles and held her tongue. Her eyes, however, were frightened for her baby, and her baby's baby. She left wads of money under my pillow or gave me checks as she kissed me goodbye.[7]

Angelou wrote these words more than 25 years ago, and we now witness a proud and distinguished woman who struggled to be her own person. Her mother wasn't always pleased with who her daughter was becoming, but we see Angelou persevering in her effort to be who she was meant to be.

Many of us can relate with the emerging Angelou. Raised in families that tell us how to feel, think, and even be, we feel strangely lost. Living someone else's life, we struggle to determine and embrace what we think or believe. Sensitive to the wishes of others, we alter our course and lose our way. Engaged in a larger church family that tells us what to believe, we are fearful of standing up and disagreeing, so we become uncertain as to what we actually believe. We are defined from the outside in rather than from the inside out.

The Legitimate Self

The idea that you can and must embrace your individuality may be news to you. The idea that you have a right, privilege, and in fact, responsibility to be uniquely you may seem beyond belief. To some, it may even sound blasphemous. It isn't.

Just as Maya Angelou fought against her mother's expectations and became her own person, so can you. The apostle Paul determined to be directed only by God, and so can you. This same legitimate sense of self can be yours. You can shamelessly take care of yourself—guilt free. You don't have to shrink back when you say no. You don't have to squirm when setting a boundary as long as you are doing so with the right motives—to take good care of yourself.

Taking care of yourself is not only your legitimate right, it is your responsibility. No one else will do it.

The Scriptures talk about the importance of treating your body as a temple of the Holy Spirit. This means that your body is sacred territory. Furthermore, the Scriptures note that all Christians have different spiritual gifts, and each one is necessary for the common good (1 Corinthians 12:7). Therefore, we shouldn't expect everyone to act the same. We must prize individuality and self-care.

No one else can or will adequately take care of you. While you wait for others to see that you are overwhelmed, life goes on. While you wait for others to see that you are angry and resentful, life goes on. While you wait for others to step in and lend a hand with your troubles, life goes on. You'll be waiting forever because *they are not responsible to take care of you.*

Some of you may be screaming, "It's not fair! I take care of their needs. Why won't they take care of mine? I tune in to them. Why don't they tune in to me?"

Although many people really are insensitive to your needs, you can find others who will be sensitive to you. However, don't confuse that with responsibility—letting others know what you need is your responsibility. You are not responsible to take care of others or to anticipate their every need. You are responsible *to care for others* but not *to take care of others.* The difference is huge.

Learning to care for others without taking care of them is a fine but radical shift for some. Learning how to desire approval without addictively seeking it will be difficult. Your task is to meet your legitimate needs as well as the legitimate needs of others.

The Legitimate Needs of Others

Learning how to be *caring* without falling prey to *caretaking* is our biggest challenge. Fortunately, the apostle Paul provides help with this task.

In Galatians, Paul says that we are to bear one another's burdens, implying that these are burdens that others cannot bear themselves. A few verses later he says, "Each one should carry his own load," referring to the burdens each one can bear himself (Galatians 6:5).

Thus, our task is to discern which burdens belong to whom. Another way to think about this is to ask, "Whose problem is this?"

Recently, I was asked by a well-meaning friend to teach a class for him at a community college on short notice. He had not adequately prepared for an absence from class that week and was in a bind. He needed a substitute, and he believed I was qualified to step in.

But I didn't really have the time to help him out. Although I wanted to help, to agree to this request would have been to do so out of a false sense of guilt and fear of his disapproval, and I would surely have felt resentment later.

Years ago, prior to my work with approval addiction recovery, I would have said yes first and dealt with the consequences later. This time, however, I said no and indicated that it would not be a good choice for me to stretch myself in this instance.

My friend was disappointed. I don't mean to sound insensitive, but that was his problem. I cannot manage others' reactions, impressions, and feelings. Trying to do this in the past has hurt me tremendously. I told my friend that if I had more notice, I could help him in the future.

Often our efforts to help others are unnecessary. We take pleasure in rescuing people, but more often than not, they don't need rescuing. In most cases, people don't need as much help as we might think they need. People can be very resourceful if we'll let them be. They find their own way out of a jam, and we're left feeling good about ourselves and about them.

Recovery from Codependency

As with all addictions, recovery from codependency requires hard work and the power of God in our lives. Let's consider several steps you can take.

First, let go of denial and grow up. Although this might sound harsh, a great deal of codependency has to do with immaturity and unrealistic expectations. Therefore, moving beyond codependency begins with acknowledging that you have some or many of these troubling traits. You must see yourself and others realistically.

Second, embrace rigorous honesty. Having let go of denial, be honest with yourself. This means facing the unpleasant aspects of your personality. Determine to control only yourself, and let go of the desire to change or please others. Ask your mate to give you feedback. Join a support group where others will offer you candid advice and evaluation.

Third, start setting healthy boundaries. Learn what is your business and what is not your business. Determine who needs your helping hand and who doesn't. Learn when and where to provide friendship and support. Additionally, commit to saying no and yes appropriately. Don't allow yourself to be victimized.

Fourth, focus on meeting your own primary needs. This doesn't mean you cannot lean on others. It means that you should not expect others to meet needs that are yours to meet. It means recognizing who you can lean on and when it is appropriate to do so.

Fifth, forgive others for disappointing you. Many people in your life have let you down or not been there for you. Forgive them. This does not mean continuing to expect the same things from them; in fact, it may mean showing "tough love" to them so that they cannot hurt you again.

Sixth, give up your need for approval. When we base our self-worth on what others think of us, we're in for a shaky ride. We must learn to please only God. Living with God's pleasure, we can then base our self-worth on our own evaluation of ourselves and on God's view of us.

Finally, trust God to do powerful work in your life. God is able to heal our wounds and bring peace to our relationships. However, we must remember that regardless of how hard we try, we cannot please all the people all the time. We must truly "let go and let God."

A Spiritual Issue

As Pia Mellody and Joyce Meyer observed, approval addiction is, in part, a spiritual condition. This addiction, like others, occurs when we become grandiose about ourselves. We struggle internally with self-esteem, but externally we act like little gods.

Walking away from the wounded gull was difficult for me. But doing so was the right move. The gull's wounds could not be fixed. Although caring was good for me, caretaking would have been a mistake.

Joyce Meyer says it like this: "There are two ways to live. We can live by grace, which is by God's favor and help, or we can live by works, which is by our own efforts, trying to do God's job. One way produces bondage, the other freedom."[8]

Codependents and approval addicts live in bondage. They burn out by trying to control others, fix them, or obtain their approval. Trying to manage something that is beyond our control is exhausting.

But what about people like Rachel, who lives every day hoping her husband will quit drinking? She cannot stop thinking about the pain he brings to their relationship. She cannot escape his sour mood, his sarcastic comments, and his inebriated condition. What is her hope?

She too must follow the healing path described earlier. She must realize that she is not God and cannot make her husband stop drinking. She must be rigorously honest with herself about his addiction and the effect it is having on her. She must develop dreams for her own life. She must address the ways she enables their destructive relationship and take appropriate steps to stop behaving in this manner. Finally, she must set healthy boundaries, which could lead her to no longer tolerate his drinking.

Do you recognize patterns of codependence and approval addiction in your own life? Are you clear about the person God has created you to be? Are you willing to be different, to disagree with others, to set healthy boundaries? If so, you're well on your way to living a life of freedom and peace.

In our final section of this book, we'll use what we've learned to face our addictions and move forward by embracing a life of recovery.

PART THREE

Naming and *Healing* Our Addictions

CHAPTER ELEVEN

Facing Our Addictions

Does not wisdom call out?
Does not understanding raise her voice?
On the heights along the way, where the paths meet,
she takes her stand.

PROVERBS 8:1-2

I KNOW THAT BAD DAYS HAPPEN, but somehow I believe they're not supposed to happen to me. Recently, I was again proven wrong.

My wife and I had decided to take a break from writing and take a play day to lie in the sand and boogey-board. Arriving at a pristine Mexican beach with sugar sand and large, rolling waves, we relaxed and read for an hour before I decided it was time to have a little fun in the surf.

Boogey board in hand, I headed toward the water. I stopped to chat with a group that was just coming out. They offered a warning about a riptide that was running hard toward the rocks to the south.

Enough said. I'd be cautious.

I danced around in the surf, acclimating myself, and then headed out. The waves were big, and I was excited about the possibility of catching a good one for a wild ride on my board.

No sooner had I gone out past waist-deep than I was yanked into deeper water. The sand shifted suddenly beneath my feet, and I completely lost my footing. I flailed wildly but could make no progress back toward shore.

I shouted for my wife, who looked on helplessly from the shore. There was nothing she could do, and she too began calling for help.

After a few moments and before anyone from the beach could reach me, I was finally able to regain my footing. Using every ounce of strength I had to battle the riptide, I fought my way back to shallow water. Breathless and frightened, I plopped down on the beach.

Christie ran to my side. "Are you all right?" she asked anxiously.

"That was scary," I replied, still panting.

"I couldn't do anything, David. I felt so helpless."

Later, I reflected on the experience. For several moments I had been completely overpowered by the riptide. If I hadn't regained my footing and if the pull hadn't let up a bit, I'd have been swept out into harsh, curling waves, into deeper water, and into deeper trouble.

I imagined this experience to be similar to what an addict feels—helplessness in the face of cravings he cannot combat. I imagined myself powerless to the pull of the tide, which could take me wherever it wanted. I was frightened, completely at the whim of forces I could not control. Similarly, the addict is at the mercy of cravings that drag him toward compulsive behaviors.

My wife and I gathered our things and headed for the safety of our hotel room. Stowing our towels and books, we settled into our car and started the engine. Before we pulled out, we shared a sigh of relief and then talked about going out to dinner when we got back to town.

Our plans were premature.

Leaving the beach, we began our trek back to town on the rutted, washed-out road. Not far from the beach, the bottom of our car struck a large rock that protruded from the roadbed. When we heard the loud scraping of the car against the rock, we both groaned.

We began losing power, and then the car lurched forward as I slowed to a stop. When we got out and looked beneath the car, we noticed a trail of pink liquid pouring from the transmission.

Climbing back into the car, we prayed that it would maintain power and stay in gear until we reached the highway, several miles away. Fortunately, we made it to the highway and even gingerly inched the car back to our hotel.

The gracious owners of the hotel calmed our frayed nerves and assisted us in dealing with the rental car company, who dispatched a replacement and arranged to have the damaged vehicle towed.

A near drowning, a damaged rental car, and an inability to speak the language. This was enough for one day.

An Uneasy Path

Facing our addictions can be much like my day in Mexico—treacherous at times, as we lose our footing and are left feeling incredibly vulnerable. The craving brain, the rituals, and the compulsions we know so well all call loudly. We're out of control, and the best we can do is point ourselves toward the beach and take one step at a time toward safe haven.

I know this doesn't sound all that encouraging, but that's the way life is when we finally confront our addictions. In fact, this is the rocky path we should expect.

You must be honest with yourself when you face your addictions: It won't be easy. Your decision to plod toward the beach through treacherous surf is enough for now. You'll make it to safety in time.

The first step is making the decision to face your addiction. It all begins with that commitment. At first, the path to freedom will feel anything but free. You'll be tempted to give up and take an easier route, which inevitably leads to disaster.

The Journey Home

Our various paths to addiction have taken us away from God and from ourselves. Facing our problems takes us on our journey home, and knowing this should provide some measure of peace. In spite of the bumpy road, we know we're heading for safe haven.

In his book *Addiction and Grace,* Gerald May reminds us, "The journey homeward, the process of homemaking in God, involves withdrawal from addictive behaviors that have become normal for us. In withdrawal, attachments are lessened and their energy is freed for simpler, purer desire and care. In other words, human desire is freed for love."[1]

Facing our addictions, according to May, means letting go of something that has become normal to us. Somehow, this is reassuring to me. I didn't sign up to become a work addict. I didn't go searching for ways to become an approval addict. But, over time, these behaviors became normal to me.

Isn't it strange how, in some fashion, our overworking, overeating, over-sexing, and over-gambling have become normal? That's why leaving these behaviors behind feels like a tremendous loss. Initially, our route to safety may seem more like an aimless road into unfamiliar territory.

These are the moments when you must trust the tiny inner voice that says, *It's time to let go of this damaging behavior and begin searching for that wonderful place I used to call "home."* In time, you'll recognize and embrace the old, familiar parts of the life you left behind.

In the beginning of my recovery from work addiction, I had the strangest dream. I dreamed that I was in a forest, dressed in work jeans, loggers' suspenders, and work boots. I was cutting firewood with a chainsaw and was covered with dirt and grease from head to toe. As I bucked a log, a salamander skittered across its surface. When I awoke, I was crying.

Because I had been in the habit of writing down my dreams, I did so in this case, though not without some discomfort. Why had this dream made me so sad? Days of reflection led me to an understanding.

By this time in my life, I had become a successful psychologist and businessman. Each day I dressed in a pressed shirt, slacks, a tie, and a sport coat. Although nothing was wrong with that, I missed *home,* an earlier time when I lived a simpler life. Back then, I cut my firewood, changed the oil in my car, raised a garden, and got my hands dirty doing honest, earthy work. (*Humus* has a close etymological connection to *human.*) Had I lost some of my humanity when I became successful?

And what about the salamander?

Salamanders change colors in response to various stimuli. They are shy and hide under rocks. Was that me? Was I afraid to go back to being the *real* David? Was I living an inauthentic life, one that had become far too mechanical and predictable?

Yes, I believe that was the case.

I let my dream simmer in my soul for a long time, contemplating about how I could "go back home." I reflected about the parts of me that had been lost to my work addiction and set out to reclaim them.

I began with baby steps. I loosened my tie and began wearing khakis to work. I took a lunch break and allowed for downtime between counseling sessions. After work I began to write, and I began cutting firewood again. I grew a garden, raised chickens, and even built a chicken coop with my sons. All were steps that carried me closer to home.

Dreams and Inspirations

My dream was instructive. The Bible is full of instances in which dreams were used to instruct and guide people. The story of Joseph is only one of many accounts in which dreams offered direction. Daniel provided the king with important messages based on his dreams. I was in good company.

Facing our addictions means finding motivation in different places. These are inspirational, instructive messages we need to hear; our addictions have silenced them for far too long. Facing our addictions is largely about facing ourselves and facing the parts of us that have gotten lost during the addictive process.

As we confront our addictions and allow ourselves to consider the path toward healing, we will inevitably need to spend time in contemplation and consideration. During these quiet moments we'll be able to do our most important work, which begins with choosing the appropriate path.

Inspiration about how to adequately face our addictions can come from many different places. During the early stages of my recovery, I received inspiration from these:

- *Dreams.* I've already shared how one dream in particular awakened a lost part of me and guided me on my journey home. Recording dreams can be a valuable way to listen to yourself and to God.

- *Journaling.* Something is powerful about sitting quietly and attending to your thoughts and feelings. In our hurried world, we rarely take time to simply pay attention to how we are feeling or to how a particular situation has affected us. Journaling offers us a time and place to be with ourselves.

- *Counseling.* Every recovery program includes a special place for professional counseling. An objective third person with expert clinical skills can be an invaluable asset as you work to put the pieces of your life back together.

- *Reading.* Scriptures and other selected reading materials can be very inspirational. Here we find "friends" who share our experiences. We find characters with whom we can relate and who awaken issues buried within us. These characters often inspire us to move forward by taking chances we wouldn't otherwise take.

- *Support groups and friends.* We all need people who will encourage us on our journey. We need safe places where we can remove our masks and let our real selves show. Simply hearing that someone else shares your addiction or struggles with the same problem can be helpful.

- *Worship.* Worship takes us out of ourselves and into the presence of God. Whether worship for you means singing joyful music or sitting quietly as the psalms are read, you can find a practice that transports you into the presence of God.

- *Prayer.* We seek contact with God, and as we do so we are changed. Find a way to pray that fits you, whether it is in silence or while listening to special music. Practice different kinds of prayer, such as praising God, listening to God, and making requests to God.

- *Change of pace.* Nothing shakes us out of our routines like a change of pace. As you begin the process of changing the destructive rituals in your life, give consideration to changing your pace. Try out new activities, new places, and new friends. Shake up your life a bit and see what happens.

We all find inspiration in different places and in different forms. As you face your addiction, consider what people and places inspire you. Discover what motivates you to take the next step in your journey toward wellness.

Reclaiming My Life

My work addiction and my recovery from it provided the crucible for my first book, *Reclaiming Manhood: A Twelve Step Journey to Becoming the Man God Wants You to Be.*

At a time when my life was falling apart, when I couldn't work as long or as hard as I'd always been able to do, I found a voice with which to express my emotional suffering. At this time I searched for a group of men to support me on my journey. Finding none, I formed my own group through contacts at my church.

What occurred every Friday for 90 minutes over the next seven years was integral to my healing. I gathered about me a troubled group of men: a burned out, workaholic pastor; a discouraged physician; an unemployed, alcoholic electrician; a young college student whose new marriage was on the rocks; and me.

We floundered during the first year or two because we were never quite sure what to talk about. Always comfortable discussing sports, we gravitated toward safer subjects. I pushed us to examine the *real* issues of our lives that we couldn't talk about elsewhere. Gradually, we became more comfortable talking about our feelings.

From those meetings, I realized the 12 steps of Alcoholics Anonymous could be used to address our problems. I decided to write a book to assist us.

I cannot adequately explain the value of that group of men to me. Alcoholics Anonymous invites anyone who wants to share "our experience, strength and hope," and this group was surely all of that to me.

A support group, functioning properly, is all of that—support—and more. The group provided me with encouragement, hope, friendship, and inspiration in overcoming my workaholism. These men helped me move beyond my work addiction and into recovery, where I experienced newfound freedom. The others in the group experienced similar support and successes.

Purpose and Intention

Facing our addictions takes great courage. We must have a clear vision about becoming healthy, along with a precise plan about how we're going to get there. We need to consciously choose to detach ourselves from our addictions one step at a time, and we need to know who and what will encourage us along the way.

We must also possess a powerful intention to break free from the bondage of addiction. We must be determined. We must fully intend to accomplish our goal of breaking our addiction.

Some people believe that the power of intention is a New Age concept. However, Jesus taught about intention when He noted the importance of counting the cost of any journey or task.

> Suppose one of you wants to build a tower. Will he not first sit down and estimate the cost to see if he has enough money to complete it? For if he lays the foundation and is not able to finish it, everyone who sees it will ridicule him, saying "This fellow began to build and was not able to finish" (Luke 14:28-32).

The psalmist promotes this perspective by encouraging us to ground our undertaking in God's plan for our lives. "Unless the LORD builds the house, its builders labor in vain" (Psalm 127:1). We can accomplish wonderful things when we cooperate with God's work.

In addition to our intention to face our addictions, we must cultivate several other attitudes and skills:

- Get clear about what you want to accomplish and then write it down. Something is powerful about putting our dreams and goals down on paper. If your goal is to break free from a food addiction, write it down. If your goal is to recover from alcoholism, write it down. This is an important step in transforming your intention into a reality.

- Set specific steps for accomplishing your goal. For example, if your objective is to be free from gambling, will you join Gamblers Anonymous or Celebrate Recovery?

- Begin taking small steps toward setting this goal into motion. Putting an action into motion is often the hardest part. Once you've developed a new routine, continuing your journey will be easier.

- Gather support from those around you—people who will encourage you to move toward your goals while holding you accountable for your progress.

- Celebrate each step in the journey. Acknowledge that your path will include small steps, giant steps, and backward steps. They are all part of the journey.

- Maintain a clear focus. Keep on keeping on. Remember that this process is a journey, not a destination!

I have found that some people fail to make progress in their recovery because they haven't planned effectively. They believe they will simply wake up one morning and say, "This is a good day to quit drinking," and somehow they will be able to follow through. They fail to take into account how difficult overcoming their addictions will be.

Detachment

Facing our addictions means facing our attachments. In fact, the word *attachment* comes from the French word *attaché,* "to be nailed to." We've been nailed to our addictions for quite some time. We stopped having the power to choose them long ago; they now choose us.

Facing our addictions means cultivating a sense of detachment. We must leave behind the familiar territory of our attachments and distance ourselves from them. We must create some breathing room, a momentary chance to regain our footing, so we can reorient ourselves and get headed toward the shore. As we begin to separate ourselves from our addictions, we gain a tiny bit of freedom with each small step we take. With each step toward detachment, our power of choice grows.

First we must detach enough to attend a 12-step meeting. Next we must connect with a clean and sober friend—someone we can trust who has possibly traveled a similar path to the one we're on. With each step, our footing becomes surer and stronger.

As we begin to distance ourselves from our addictions, we leave room to practice some of the forms of inspiration offered earlier. Through these tools and through the practice of detachment, we loosen the grip of the addiction and strengthen God's hold on our life.

Withdrawal

Facing your addictions means going through pain. I wish it weren't so. I wish we could simply recognize a bad habit, stop it in its tracks, and whisk it away with the swipe of the hand.

But that's not the way it works. We're attached to our addictions. They seem normal to us. We've integrated them into our lives. Prying ourselves loose from our addictions and facing them head-on will be a huge challenge. We must anticipate some discomfort. Gerald May speaks to the role of loss in the process of facing our addictions:

> The loss of attachment is the loss of something very real; it is physical. We will resist this loss as long as we possibly can. When withdrawal does happen, it will hurt. And, after it is over, we will mourn. Only then, when we have completed the grieving over our lost attachment, will we breathe the fresh air of freedom with appreciation and gratitude.[2]

Confronting our addictions and preparing for this journey of recovery must include preparing for loss and sadness. It will also include resistance because we don't want to give up this deep-rooted attachment. In fact, if we could find any way around it, we'd take it. If you've tried to let go of an addiction while refusing to endure the accompanying pain, you already know that it doesn't work. But that didn't stop us from trying.

Elizabeth Kübler-Ross, famed author of a seminal work on the stages of loss titled *On Death and Dying,* said we all go through various stages when letting go of our attachments.

- We have *denial* about our need to even go through the grief process.
- Then we experience *anger* about the necessity of facing our addiction.
- We attempt to *bargain* our way out of having to accept this loss.
- We then settle into the reality of our need to let go of our addiction and feel *depressed* as a result.
- Finally, perhaps out of sheer exhaustion, we reach a place of serenity called *acceptance.*

Although I find Dr. Ross' work helpful, I believe that very few people move through these stages in a linear fashion—I certainly didn't. Just when I thought I was reaching a place of acceptance, my old friend denial would return for a visit and whisper, *You don't really have to quit working so hard, David. You've got a handle on this thing.*

Right!

Then I'd slip into a mild depression, saddened and discouraged that denial had led me astray. The problem was severe, and I remained in recovery for a long time. Two steps forward, one step back. Or at times, one step forward and two steps back.

I call it *herky-jerky recovery.* That's the way it worked for me. Acceptance seems to come and go and is not simply a stage we settle into. Before you make friends with acceptance, you will likely need to go through the other stages more than once.

Let Go, Let God

Many of you will recognize "Let go and let God" as a foundational tool for nearly every kind of recovery program. Facing our addictions includes grabbing hold of another applicable cliché: "Your best thinking got you here."

In other words, if my best efforts landed me smack dab in the middle of a work and approval addiction, I'm surely not going to be able to single-handedly pull myself out of this mess. If all my wisdom assisted me in being a workaholic for 20 years, in spite of countless others who tried to help me see the light, I'd be a fool to decide that I am smart enough, wise enough, strong enough, and brave enough to find my way home alone.

It's not going to happen.

So, then what?

We must decide not to go it alone.

We must admit our utter dependence on God. We need God more than anything. We gather support from those around us to assist us when the going gets rough, and we must also lean on Jesus, our higher power, to shine the light on the dark trail ahead.

We discover we can't trust our best thinking, and we find that we've got to check our thinking against Scripture and share our thoughts and feelings with the few people we've gathered to support us on our journey. We let go of one of the most dangerous demons around—our grandiosity.

Our best thinking, something most addicts spend a great deal of time cultivating, reaches extremes of grandiosity—a fancy word meaning, "I can figure it out. I've got it knocked, and I don't need help from others and certainly don't need to rely on God to get me out of this mess."

When you hear this inner voice, I encourage you to run, not walk, away from it. Grandiosity is not your friend. Grandiosity is the cousin of denial, and the two spend far too much time together. Leave them behind as quickly as possible.

The Consecrated Journey

Agreeing that we must "let go and let God" by giving up our independence and grandiosity, we depend on His strength to keep us on track throughout our journey. We can't fight this fight alone. Fierce, stubborn independence got us into a lot of trouble. We must return to a dependence on God and add to this dependence a consecration of our journey to Him.

What is the consecrated journey? It means recognizing both the immensity of this undertaking and the fact that we can do only what we can do and no more. Where we end is where God begins. When our best efforts are limited, God's are not. So with an eye on the road ahead, I ask you to consecrate your journey to God. I encourage you to ask God to create a space within you and to fill it with His grace.

For now, it is enough that you have begun the journey. This is a mighty step. You have mapped out a plan and are determined to endure the pain of withdrawal. You are prepared to throw off the bondage of addiction and embrace the freedom of recovery.

Whatever your addiction may be, remember that we all can champion one another. We all know how hard letting go can be. We know how much easier it would be to hang on to our debilitating habits, but we also recognize that this is not a healthy path for us. Together we choose recovery. Together we ask God to consecrate our journey toward recovery and to provide us with His grace along the way.

Consecration includes asking God to make something holy out of our mess. It also means believing that He'll do so. "And we know that in all things God works for the good of those who love him, who have been called according to his purpose" (Romans 8:28).

Our final two chapters will outline additional strategies for making a successful escape from our addictions and a successful transition into recovery. We'll examine where the road is likely to get rough, how relapse can occur, and what to do when it does.

Let's move forward together on the path to recovery.

CHAPTER TWELVE

Letting Go

*Through loyalty to the past, our mind refuses to realize
that tomorrow's joy is possible only if today's makes way for it;
that each wave owes the beauty of its line
only to the withdrawal of the receding one.*

ANDRÉ GIDE

I REMEMBER THE STORY about the greedy monkey who reaches into the jar filled with colorful candy and grabs a handful. With his fist full of candy, he can no longer pull his hand out. He tugs and tugs, but regardless of how hard he tries, his hand won't come out. Not until he loosens his grip on the candy will he be free.

I feel like this monkey at times. I wrap my hands around something—like a work project—that looks good to me at the time, but later I feel trapped by it.

"Oooh, another speaking engagement!" I exclaim to my wife.

"Sounds great," she says, "but where are you going to fit it into your schedule?" she asks soberly. "You'd have to let go of something else."

I pause for a moment to consider her question and comment. Of course she is right, and I must give something up to invite some new activity into my life.

"I don't know," I say, reluctant to let go of *my* brightly colored candy—work.

My heart goes out to the monkey. I felt like this monkey during my work addiction days, clinging to the work that was killing me. Greedy with work and exciting projects, I refused to let go. I was caught in my own trap, like the monkey with its hand in the jar.

Letting Go

The principle of letting go is central to any addiction recovery program. Most recovery programs, in fact, include some aspect of letting go and letting God. More to the point, they stress the importance of letting go of the addictive substance or behavior and of our old way of living so we can experience freedom. We must open our hands, eyes, and heart to a new way of thinking and living. We call this *recovery*. Don't be misled, however, as this is a process, not an event. It is much easier said than done.

The monkey is trapped because of its refusal to let go. Looking at the poor monkey, we want to say, "Let go of the candy. You'll die if you don't."

"No," the monkey might say. "I want it all. I need it all. I'm going to hang on to it."

"But," we persist, "you'll remain stuck and die. Trust me. Let go of the candy, and your hand will slip right out."

We are in no position, however, to preach to the monkey because we too cling tenaciously to our addictions. We know we're eating too much, and soon our eating becomes an addiction, and the food has us in a stranglehold. We know our gambling is gaining a larger foothold on our life, and we can't let go.

We can see the addiction in others. We want to scream, "Let go! Give it up!" We offer quick fixes and clichés for solutions. On the inside, however, where we grapple with the cravings, life is much more difficult. Clichés about letting go are not so helpful.

William Bridges, author of *The Way of Transitions,* says this about letting go: "We don't let go of anything important until we have exhausted all the possible ways that we might keep holding onto it."[1]

Bridges says we try to bargain our way into holding on to the valued process or substance if there is any way possible to do so. We bargain with ourselves, others, and even God to find a way to hang on to our old way of living. We must often exhaust ourselves or experience some kind of breakdown before we can admit our addiction and need for recovery.

As I've said before, we must have a breakdown before we can have a breakthrough. We all wish we could learn lessons the easy way, without any cost or loss, but our addictions are far too complex for this. I had to learn my lessons about work and approval from my emotions—times of discouragement and exhaustion. I didn't listen to my father or friends who warned me about the dangers of my workaholism.

Perhaps like me, you've struggled to let go. You've maintained your fierce independence, determined to do things your way. Perhaps like me, you've begun to see that your old way of doing things isn't working.

Surrender

If rigidly hanging on to old ways of doing things is futile, and dogged determination to old ways of thinking leads to more confusion, what must you do to let go and loosen the grip of addiction in your life? What does it mean to release your grip on the colorful candy?

Before we can reach the promised land of acceptance—which is our goal in winning our war over addiction—we must grapple with surrender. We have to see and experience firsthand that what we're doing is not working. It's worse than not working—it's ruining us. Only then will we face the possibility of defeat.

We've grown up hearing, however, that defeat is intolerable. Letting go is for cowards. We don't give up in a high school fight or in a competitive sporting event. But in the business of facing and healing our addictions, surrender is anything but a cowardly response. It is the courageous work of a hero.

Submission precedes surrender, and surrender precedes acceptance. Submission is a beginning step, usually with a large dose of denial still mixed in. We recognize that what we're doing isn't working, but we don't realize the severity of our problems. We're all addicts, familiar with this kind of fuzzy thinking. It sounds like this:

- "I know my pornography use is a problem, and I'll cut back on it. I've got it under control."

- "Sure, my gambling is excessive, but I'm not addicted. I'll only gamble a day or two a week, and I'll limit my spending."

- "My spending has been out of control, but I can manage it now. I'm going to control my spending, but I'm not going to give up my credit cards."

- "I know I shouldn't worry about what everyone thinks of me, but I can't help it. I'm sure not going to counseling for it."

Brennan Manning, a favorite author of mine, makes a critical distinction for us. Manning, a recovering alcoholic who is keenly familiar with hanging on to old behaviors, explains the difference between submission and surrender in his book *Reflections for Raga-muffins*. He helps us see we can let go of a behavior without really having a heart transformation: "It is important to note that submission is not surrender. The former is the acceptance of reality consciously, not unconsciously. There is a superficial yielding, but tension continues."

How can we know if we have moved from submission to surrender? Manning continues: "When the Christian surrenders to the Spirit on the unconscious level, there is no residual battle, and relaxation ensues with freedom from strain and conflict. Submission, on the other hand, is half-hearted acceptance."[2]

Halfhearted acceptance, or half measures, will not get you to the other side of addiction. Saying you've hit the bottom and are ready for change, fingers crossed behind your back, fools no one. Submission, according to Manning, is a meager concession tainted with denial.

And so it goes. Halfhearted admissions. Recognizing there is a problem but refusing to fully surrender to the challenge of recovery. We can never recover if we don't vigorously strive for an attitude of surrender.

If half measures equal submission, what does full surrender look like?

Surrender is an integral concept of step one of Alcoholics Anonymous and vital to our recovery: "We admitted that we were powerless over alcohol—that our lives had become unmanageable."

The apostle Paul hit his bottom and reached surrender when he said, "I know nothing good lives in me, that is, in my sinful nature. For I have the desire to do what is good, but I cannot carry it out" (Romans 7:18).

Surrender is an attitude void of denial and critical to healing our addictions. We admit that our lives are unmanageable. We let go of bargaining with our spouse, our boss, ourselves, and God. We look critically in the mirror and admit, at the deepest level possible, that we cannot continue to live the way we are living. Our life is not working. Our addictions are killing us.

Dedication to Reality

Scott Peck, in his book *The Road Less Traveled*, says a critical discipline to any kind of change is dedication to the truth, which involves surrendering to the unmanageability of our lives. Peck knows that surrender is the path to acceptance, and acceptance is the path to healing our addiction. He notes that seeking the truth...

> must be continually employed if our lives are to be healthy and our spirits are to grow...The more clearly we see the reality of the world, the better equipped we are to deal with the world. The less clearly we see the reality of the world—the more our minds are befuddled by falsehood, misperceptions and illusions—the less able we will be to determine correct courses of action and make wise decisions.[3]

If you're anything like me, you're saying, "I'm willing to face the truth. I know I need to change. But..."

And the bargaining begins.

"But..."

You hold back from surrendering to the truth.

"But..."

I'm working with a young professional woman, both charming and industrious. Lynn works for one of the large banks in town, managing 25 people. With an MBA from a prestigious university, she has risen quickly in the business world. But she's not happy. She's 100 pounds overweight and frustrated with her continual failed attempts to reduce.

I initially thought our work would be straightforward. She'd begin the process of facing her addiction, and she'd be open to suggestions about changing her fast-food eating habits and the importance of exercise. But as soon as we began discussing the cost of change and her need to surrender to the power of her addiction, she began missing appointments and making excuses for not changing her lifestyle.

I didn't immediately confront Lynn on her obvious resistance, still thinking she'd begin to acknowledge her eating disorder. She

verbalized her frustration and voiced her sadness and discouragement that she could manage a bank but couldn't remain focused
and dedicated to losing weight.

I shared with Lynn the power of addictions.

"Your brain craves certain kinds of foods, Lynn," I said. "You're
going to have to face those cravings and manage them."

"Yeah, I know all that," she said abruptly. "But, it shouldn't be
this hard to lose weight. I've cut back on the sweets I used to eat all
the time."

"That's a great start, but it will take more than that," I said. "What
do you think about adding an exercise component to your life?"

"I hate going to a gym," she said angrily.

"Why is that?"

"I just don't want to get dressed up in little shorts and a T-shirt
and look stupid."

"I don't understand," I said.

"No offense," she said, "but you're a guy and wouldn't understand. Women don't want to go a gym and sweat. I don't have the
time to do it anyway."

"Losing weight is going to be hard work," I said. "It takes fully
understanding your body, your cravings, and what it will take for
you to lose the weight you want."

I watched Lynn's eyes turn away. I sensed her resistance; I could
feel her pull away. I listened as she rationalized that she should be
able to lose weight without having to join a gym or participate in
a support group.

There it was. She wouldn't face the truth of her situation. She
wanted to maintain control. She wanted to hang on to vestiges
of her eating style, which obviously wasn't working for her. She
had not hit her bottom, and she wasn't yet willing to let go and
face the enormity of her problem. She wasn't willing to surrender
to her addiction. Like the monkey with its hand in the jar, Lynn
clung to her old ways, and they were killing her self-esteem and
self-confidence.

Three months later, Lynn weighed the same as the first day she walked in my door for counseling. More important, however, her mind-set remained the same: She refused to surrender to the severity of her problem. She refused to listen to my confrontation of her denial and attachment to old ways of living. She remains dedicated to her distorted view of reality. I see a dismal future for her.

Parable of the Rich Young Man

Jesus speaks to us about the importance of letting go and surrendering to a new path. So much of Jesus' teaching involved letting go of our attachment to this world and inviting a new viewpoint to enter and change our lives. His experience with a rich young man is illustrative.

> As Jesus started on his way, a man ran up to him and fell on his knees before him. "Good teacher," he asked, "what must I do to inherit eternal life?"
>
> "Why do you call me good?" Jesus answered. "No one is good—except God alone. You know the commandments: 'Do not murder, do not commit adultery, do not steal, do not give false testimony, do not defraud, honor your father and mother.'"
>
> "Teacher," he declared, "all these I have kept since I was a boy."
>
> Jesus looked at him and loved him. "One thing you lack," he said. "Go, sell everything you have and give to the poor, and you will have treasure in heaven. Then come, follow me."
>
> At this the man's face fell. He went away sad, because he had great wealth (Mark 10:17-22).

We can feel the man's discouragement. He's been working hard to be a good person, rigidly keeping the laws and commandments. He really believes he's done everything Jesus asked of him. But Jesus sees his heart and the fact that he is still clinging to one thing—his treasure here on earth. Jesus sees he is trapped by his possessions and wants him to be free. He asks the man to surrender, and the challenge is too great.

I can't help comparing this man to you and me. We want God's blessings but won't surrender our grasp on the candy. We want freedom but don't want to pay too high a price for it. Are we ready to let go of the candy?

No Wavering

Facing our addictions and healing them require a clear focus, determination, incredible courage, and sure faith. They require an unwavering dedication to the truth and to surrendering our old life.

The story of the rich young man reminds me of the apostle James' admonition on the importance of facing the truth and being clear minded.

"He who doubts is like a wave of the sea, blown and tossed by the wind. That man should not think he will receive anything from the Lord; he is a double-minded man, unstable in all he does" (James 1:6-8).

During my workaholic years, I was like a small ship bobbing about on a violent ocean. One day I was determined to live a balanced life. The very next day, I determined to push myself harder to achieve more money, prestige, and accumulations. One day I was spiritually minded, ready to give myself over to the power of God, and the next day I was ready to steer my life in whatever direction pleased me. Double minded and doubtful, my life was out of control.

"Blown and tossed by the wind"—that describes my pre-recovery life. I was dedicated to work, not to reality or to my faith. Subsequently, I wavered in my life direction. As if I were frantically gripping the rudder of my boat, I "white-knuckled" my efforts to cut back on work, hoping my life would reach calm waters. I used willpower to make modest changes but quickly slipped back into my workaholism. I needed to let go of half measures and to face the truth of my life.

Surrendering to a life of recovery requires letting go of our old way of doing things and reaching forward with faith toward a new life.

This sounds far easier than it is. I was reminded recently that I am *recovering* from my workaholism; I am not *recovered*. On a night out recently, Christie caught me nervously looking down at my cell phone.

"Would you please turn off your phone?" she asked, notably upset.

"I'm expecting an important business call," I answered defensively.

"Can't it wait until after dinner, or even tomorrow?"

Annoyed, I turned off my phone, but not before shooting her a look of irritation.

After a few tense moments I apologized to her. Of course, asking me to turn off my phone was reasonable. Certainly she deserved my undivided attention. In fact, I'm embarrassed that I even had to be asked for such a simple courtesy. The tentacles of work addiction had crept back into my life, and I needed to take another honest inventory of the situation.

The struggle didn't end there, however. I turned off my phone, all right, but I didn't turn off my brain. I still *wanted* to check my phone for messages. I still *wondered* if that call had come through. Christie didn't have my full attention. I remained a double-minded man, espousing one set of principles while living another. I had submitted but hadn't surrendered. I had given in to her request, but my heart was not fully changed.

Are you tossed about like the waves on the sea? Have you "white-knuckled" yourself into submission, using sheer willpower to wrestle with your addiction without fully surrendering?

Full surrender is the beginning of real transformation. The process starts with a change of behavior, continues with a change of mind, and ends with a change of heart. Full surrender leads to full acceptance, the basis for healing our addictions.

Facing Our Fear

Relinquishing control of our lives and surrendering to a higher power (God) can be a very scary process. We know what life is like with our attachments. What will it be like when we let go?

Many of us everyday addicts live compulsively. With us, it's all-or-nothing. We're extreme people who want complete control of our lives. Full surrender, which is absolutely necessary for healing, means letting go of life the way we live it. It means facing the fear of letting go of our addiction as well as facing new fears that are likely to crop up.

Melody Beattie, author of *The Language of Letting Go,* says we all are afraid of letting go of the illusion of power we feel over our lives. Real power, she asserts, comes from facing our fears and surrendering.

"Surrendering to a Power greater than ourselves is how we become empowered. We become empowered in a new, better, more effective way than we believed possible."[4]

Prior to surrendering my addictions and new life to God, I was exhausted and confused. Though weary, I still clung tenaciously to my old workaholic life. Tensions had risen to a high pitch in my marriage, and my concentration suffered, but I didn't want to let go. I still feared letting go of my old life, being uncertain as to what a new life might look like. I knew my "old self" and was uncertain as to what this "new self" would look like.

I began journaling furiously.

- "I'm afraid to go to counseling. I'm supposed to have it all together."
- "What will I learn about myself in counseling? What will I have to change?"

- "I'm afraid to open up to these men in the men's group. What if they think my fears are crazy?"
- "What is going to happen to my private practice if I quit taking new referrals?"
- "I feel like a failure. I should be able to handle everything, and I can't."

I had to face these fears and more. I spent years in counseling, talking about my childhood and my relationships with my parents and siblings. I explored my relationship to work and money. I examined my greed, my need to add more things to my life, and I discovered a superficial effort to control my world. I talked and talked, and gradually, over time, I surrendered my old life, creating space for a new one.

Feel the Fear and Do It Anyway

We all have fears. When we become honest with ourselves, we will face these fears and move forward. One step at a time. One decision at a time.

But what about the issue of choice? Haven't I said in this book that when it comes to recovery, our ability to choose is compromised?

Yes. It is compromised, but it's not negated completely.

So what can we choose to do?

We can, by facing our fears, choose recovery. We can choose to enter a treatment program that deals specifically with our addiction. We can choose to participate in Celebrate Recovery, a Christian-based recovery group for all addictions. We can choose to tell others about our addiction. We can choose to read everything we can find about our addiction and recovery, including the Scriptures.

Each of these steps requires facing our fears. Remember, addiction doesn't want to be exposed. Addiction doesn't want recovery, doesn't want a new way of life, doesn't want the power of God to influence it.

So fear may be a companion on our journey. Any new and unknown path is likely to include discomfort. We must expect to have fear at times.

Susan Jeffers, author of the book *Feel the Fear and Do It Anyway* says, "The 'doing it' comes *before* the feeling better about yourself. When you make something happen, not only does the fear of the situation go away, but also you get a big bonus: you do a lot toward building self-confidence."[5]

Feeling our fears and "doing it anyway" is a powerful behavior to add to our lives. Taking on new challenges and succeeding creates self-confidence, which we use to tackle the next hurdle. And self-confidence is a wonderful antidote to fear. Self-confidence is greatly bolstered when we have a powerful connection to the author of courage—God.

The Scriptures remind us, "For God did not give us a spirit of timidity, but a spirit of power, of love and of self-discipline" (2 Timothy 1:7).

We're also reminded, "No temptation has seized you except what is common to man. And God is faithful; he will not let you be tempted beyond what you can bear. But when you are tempted, he will also provide a way out so that you can stand up under it" (1 Corinthians 10:13).

Nothing you are struggling with is new. We're a group of everyday addicts. Your addiction may look a little different from mine, but I know the struggle you're experiencing. Others know your struggle too. Our path to freedom is to face our fears, take one step at a time, and discover the peace that comes from surrender and acceptance.

Acceptance

We've all experienced the power of addictions and the craving brain. We've used our willpower to rail against our addictions. We've fought and struggled, clawed and scratched our way to reach temporary lessening of the craving brain, only to have the urges come roaring back, stronger than ever. We've been tough, strong, willful, and perhaps even defiant. Even so, the cravings return, and we fall back into old patterns and habits. We feel discouraged and defeated with our erratic progress. We wonder if there is any hope for us. Will we ever find relief from the craving brain?

Yes. As we fully embrace the power of surrender and acceptance, we find peace. As we cultivate this powerful attitude in our lives, we find healing. Acceptance is not only helpful, it is mandatory. Acceptance is the doorway leading to a brand-new life.

No longer ashamed and hiding, we accept the unmanageability of our lives and surrender our will and life over to the power of God. We face the reality that our addiction is killing us and that we've been unsuccessful at taming the urgings on our own. We accept that we must enter into recovery, whatever form that might take.

We walk the tightrope between being powerless in our addiction and embracing the power of God in our lives to at least make some small choices—to go to that first Alcoholics Anonymous or Celebrate Recovery meeting or other support group. We begin to understand that powerlessness over the craving brain doesn't mean we sit back and wallow in our addiction. We have the power to make some healing decisions.

Acceptance means having the courage to stare our addiction down—we accept the power of our addiction and the debilitating impact it has on our lives. We're willing to consider the many people we've hurt by our addiction, including ourselves. Accepting our humanity, we move ahead with clarity about our particular addiction.

Acceptance doesn't mean that we berate ourselves for our failures. We feel a healthy sense of sadness over our past choices. Like David, we feel sad and contrite. "The sacrifices of God are a broken spirit; a broken and contrite heart, O God, you will not despise" (Psalm 51:17). We're willing to make amends to people we have harmed.

Acceptance also means discovering a new attitude of

self-acceptance. Knowing that God honors our honesty, our efforts, and the humility of having failed, we can walk tall. Gone are the secrets. We're finished with the lies as well as our double-minded wavering. By relinquishing ourselves to the care of God, we achieve strength and courage to move forward.

Acceptance is far more than admitting failure. It is also the beginning of an incredible journey. This can be an exciting time in our lives as we embrace new possibilities. Facing and healing our addiction means we have an opportunity for a new life. Another chance. Another possibility for the kind of life we want to live. We no longer fearfully shrink from change, but invite it into our lives with a sense of wonder and excitement.

No Pain, No Gain

One of the primary obstacles to surrender and acceptance is the pain it reveals in our lives. When we truly admit that our lives have become unmanageable and that we've hurt ourselves and many others, we come face-to-face with that pain and sadness. If we're not careful, this sadness can pervade our lives and smother us.

We must feel our emotions but not be overwhelmed by them. This is a new skill for most of us because in the past we dealt with emotional pain by anesthetizing our feelings with more of the addictive substance or process that made our lives unmanageable in the first place.

The only sure way out is to feel and embrace our pain.

"Why would I want to feel this shame, guilt, anger, and intense sadness?" one woman asked me. Participating in my parenting class as a requirement to have her children returned to her after years of neglect, she was understandably frightened.

Susan's voice quivered as she softly said, "Lord knows I already feel bad enough without staring at my failures. I hate the years I spent using drugs and alcohol. I can't stand to think about what I put my kids through."

"Yes," I said, "I understand. But as we face any loss—and our years of addiction are filled with losses—we have feelings about those losses. If we deny those feelings, we'll likely search for old ways to numb them, sending us back into our addictive behaviors."

"So I have to wallow in guilt and shame?" she asked sarcastically.

"We never have to wallow in guilt or shame," I said. "But we do have to develop self-awareness, learning to acknowledge what our addiction and behaviors mean to us and those we love."

She looked at me, still obviously puzzled. She'd been overwhelmed by her sadness, guilt, and shame before. Then she anesthetized her feelings by using drugs and alcohol. Neither option worked effectively.

And so our answer is to learn to accept our addiction and begin the process of feeling our feelings. Nothing else—just feeling our feelings. Not running from them. Not overanalyzing them. Not trying to make complete sense of them. Just feeling them, naming them, and beginning the gentle exploration of what these feelings ask of us.

Tears welled up in Susan's eyes as she shared about the many times she'd allowed her children to fend for themselves while she went searching for drugs. She felt intense guilt about the days when she plopped them in front of the television, too hungover to care for them.

"Grief is the healing feeling," I reminded her. "Stay with your feelings, and soon enough they will dissipate. You are accepting the gravity of your addiction and moving toward a new and wonderful life."

Susan had much work to do before her children would be returned to her. She was reluctantly willing to face her pain. This would be her only true path toward acceptance and healing.

As Susan moves forward into recovery, Lynn still struggles with her weight, clinging to the belief that she can lose weight without changing her life or thoughts. She's still searching for a shortcut, feeling discouraged by her lack of progress. She has yet to surrender to the power of her eating addiction. She has yet to feel the pain that will come if she tells herself the truth—that half measures of recovery won't work. That she has to change how she eats and begin to exercise. She has yet to face the fact that the willpower she uses in her business won't conquer her eating addiction.

Lynn has yet to face the pain her addiction causes her. She avoids those feelings, preferring to pretend she is in control of her life. She feels sad but not sad enough to change. She feels discouraged but not discouraged enough to change.

Susan and Lynn both need to face their lives honestly and grieve. They must grieve not only for past choices but also for their lives, which must change if they are to move beyond addiction. Without the pain that comes with acceptance they cannot move further along on their journey. If they experience this pain, they can move into full acceptance of their addiction and continue forward with healing.

Transformation

As we fully experience and accept our current situation, we open up to the possibility of a new life with new opportunities. We embrace the scriptural principle that God can use anything for the good of those who love Him and whom He has called (Romans 8:28). All things can be beneficial. We no longer feel shame over our addiction. Having accepted our addiction, we're now able to use our energies to seek and embrace recovery, to discover the new life God has for us.

Accepting our addiction, rather than dancing around the truth, is our pathway into a new life. We will no longer settle for superficial, quick fixes—we seek true and lasting transformation. As we cooperate with God in this process, this Scripture becomes a description of our lives: "Therefore, if anyone is in Christ, he is a new creation; the old is gone, the new has come!" (2 Corinthians 5:17).

Changed from the inside out, we become new creations with new attitudes. We gain freedom from the old, craving brain and move forward into our new life of freedom—recovery. We move forward to healing our addictions.

> I have come out of the past five years with great sympathy for people who toss in the towel and try either to retreat back into some old security (addiction) or to fast forward through change (any change!) that will make their lives different. But, having chose neither of those options, I have gained a new sense of myself—a sense based much less on my ability to think things through than on purely subjective experience of being the one to whom my life was happening.[6]

William Bridges shares these words about the excruciating loss of his wife, though he could have easily been talking about our addictions. Bridges deals with a different kind of transition, but ours has many similarities. We too are tempted to retreat, clutching onto our old life rather than reach toward our new one.

For us to enter the realm of recovery, we must accept that we have an addiction, that our lives have become unmanageable. We must admit that our own wisdom propelled us further down the road of destruction. We learn that for now, we must trust others to lead us out of this wilderness.

We grab hold of acceptance. We accept that we are powerless over drugs, alcohol, or any other addiction. We acknowledge deep within that our addiction leads to only one thing—death. Emotional, spiritual, and possibly even physical death. We surrender our lives and, with renewed self-acceptance, enter recovery. We surrender our will and lives over to the care of God, recognizing that He will lead and guide us not only into sobriety but also into transformation.

Acceptance is a choice you can make today. This powerful choice leads to rediscovering yourself and integrating all your losses and failures into a beautiful new mosaic that pleases God. It's your choice. Acceptance leads you into powerful healing from your addiction.

Let's now explore how we can heal fully from our addiction. We'll explore how to prevent relapse and what to do if relapse occurs. We'll learn how to live a life of recovery from addiction.

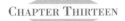

CHAPTER THIRTEEN

Healing Our Addictions

Out of the depths I cry to you, O LORD; O LORD, hear my voice.
Let your ears be attentive to my cry for mercy.

PSALM 130:1-2

I AM AN ADDICT. Most of us are.

That's where we started this book, and that's where we'll end. Openly stating that I'm an addict is the first and most powerful step I can take. All of our future work is grounded in the admission that our lives have become unmanageable and that we need help.

In this book, I've devoted a great deal of time to the topic of denial because it is our biggest enemy. Denial takes many forms, and like poison ivy that has recently been pruned, it is forever trying to creep back into our lives.

Denial's most virile and deadly form comes when I insist that I don't have an addiction. This leads to emotional, spiritual, and sometimes even physical death. Denial allows our addiction to spread like an untreated cancer, invading and eating away at more and more aspects of our life.

Denial also takes a milder form as minimization when I tell myself, *I've got a problem, but I'm no addict. It's not that serious.* This road also leads to tragedy and self-destruction.

Finally, denial can also take the form of acknowledging I have a problem while insisting I can fix the problem myself. Even as the "cancer" spreads, too many of us cling tenaciously to the following rationale: *I can quit by myself. I don't need any fancy tools, support groups, or professional psycho-babble. Willpower is my medicine.* It's a different type of denial, but it takes us down the same path as the others.

I hope you've conquered your denial by now. I hope you've come to a place where you can admit that you are a card-carrying member of our grand parade of addicts and that your addiction is a virulent disease. In the past, we've tried to perform surgery on ourselves and botched the job. We've tried to minimize the problem, but this has done nothing to eradicate it. The problem is larger than our ability to solve it. We're addicts, and we need intervention.

Intervention

Our change in direction comes in the form of an intervention, a barrier across our path that tells us we can go no further. This is the end of the road. When we reach this point, recovery can begin.

For some, that barrier is a legal charge, such as a DUI, shouting that our drinking is out of control. For some, it is a spouse saying that unless we enter treatment, he or she is leaving. For others, such as myself, it is sheer exhaustion; we can no longer keep up the pace and the lifestyle. We are ready to surrender.

Intervention means we're not going to keep doing what we've always done while expecting different results. We're going to humble ourselves and seek help. We're going to change!

Keep in mind that this change won't come without a fight. We're attached to our old ways of doing things, even though we live in chaos, unpredictability, and confusion. You might think that we'd eagerly abandon this sinking ship, but that's not the way addicts operate. We have our old rituals, our craving brain and behavior patterns that have become powerful parts of who we are. Letting go is not easy.

Intervention begins as an external barrier, but if things go well we internalize the change process. Slowly, sometimes with much resistance, we accept the importance of healthy change. We accept a path recommended to us by someone who has extensive knowledge about the road we are traveling. Intervention means looking long and hard at what we've been doing and asking for help from others who know more than we know.

Does this mean that I need to reach out for help? Yes.

Do I have to admit that what I've been doing isn't working? Precisely.

Will I have to admit that I need a hand from someone who is knowledgeable about this kind of problem? Yep.

Will I really have to relinquish some control over my life? That's right.

Let me put it to you in very simple terms. If you keep doing what you've always done, you're going to get what you've always gotten. This is not rocket science. On the other hand, if you try something new, you stand a chance of changing old behaviors, rituals, and compulsive actions.

Interventions are often initiated by a friend or family member. If you're the mate or friend of an addict, stop going along with the traditional game plan. You have the power to erect a barrier in the middle of the road to destruction. Look closely at the ways you may be enabling a destructive process to continue, and vow to stop it.

In the midst of my emotional collapse from workaholism, my therapist advised my family to start treating me differently. He encouraged them to voice their dissatisfaction with my long work hours. He encouraged them to share their feelings and challenge me about my unhealthy choices. Although this didn't immediately change my behavior, their behavior and feelings were key ingredients in the process that led me to transform my life.

After I'd become completely exhausted, my therapist challenged me to change my life, one step at a time. The external motivation eventually became internalized. He advised me to change my work schedule and begin adding some enjoyable activities to my life. Because I trusted him and knew that I desperately needed help, I gave his suggestions a try. And gradually—very, very gradually—I began feeling better. The domino effect of healing began to make a difference in my life. An external intervention (my exhaustion) became an internal motivation to change.

How can you apply the concept of intervention to your life right now? If you're married to an addict, stop enabling the destructive process. Stop throwing up your hands and saying you can do nothing to inhibit your mate's drinking. You can do plenty. Make a list of the ways you make it easy for him to continue with his addiction. Stop those behaviors, one by one.

Next, make a list of how you can begin behaving differently. Shake things up a bit. Let him know you won't ride in a car with him when he's been drinking. Let her know that you won't make love if she's under the influence of illicit drugs. Commit to going to church each and every Sunday. Stop doing the things you've always done that help a loved one to continue living a life of addiction.

If you are the mate of an addict, you'll probably need professional counseling to pull this off. You're probably more caught up in the addictive process than you realize. Get a professional's input regarding ways you can intervene in the life of an addict, and trust the professional to lead you out of the wilderness.

If you are an addict, you're going to have a very difficult time leading another addict into the promised land. Get help with your own problems first, and then you'll be in a better position to provide intervention to your mate.

In some cases, we see interventions on a grand scale, where friends and families, guided by a trained professional, let the addict know the impact the addictive behavior is having on them. These can be incredibly powerful and transformational times as a family gathers around the addict and announces that they will no longer support, enable, or interact with them as they have in the past.

No Fancy Tricks

As I prepared to write this final chapter, I felt very fragile, even discouraged and powerless, because I'm painfully aware that fancy tricks and gimmicks will not cure you of your addiction. Yes, intervention is a wonderful tool, but beyond that, what can I offer? The bottom line is that breaking free from an addiction is no easy matter.

We're still learning how addictions are formed and how people can recover from them. We know the craving brain will act like a riptide, dragging us out into dangerous waters. The statistics on complete recoveries from addictions, without relapse, are pessimistic. I wish it weren't so.

Not only are there no fancy tricks and no absolute cures, but the few tools we all agree are critical only lessen our chances of relapse by a small degree. They are, nonetheless, critically important steps to take.

However, as Scott Peck said in his book *The Road Less Traveled,* facing this truth can be empowering. When we acknowledge the fact that our path to recovery includes legitimate suffering, and when we take on and endure that suffering, we become better, stronger.

No fancy tricks. No quick-fix gimmicks. Just the difficult but satisfying work of recovery.

So, what do I have to offer?

Here's what I can do. I'll share the tools I've found to be most helpful during my healing journey, and I'll remind you that there are no magic bullets, fancy tricks, or potions. In fact, only rarely—and I've seen it happen only once or twice—is anyone miraculously cured of all their cravings and urges. For that reason, we would be wise not to count on a miracle.

Most importantly, I can offer effective steps for healing—and prayers for grace from our Lord. We'll hold hands as we cross the street. We'll encourage one another. We'll pray for each other.

So let's get to it. Let's grab hold of the practices that will help us during the recovery process.

Desire for Recovery

In order to take on our addictions and maintain a steady course on the healing path, we must truly want recovery. Intention is half the battle, but we must combine it with a strong dose of desire. We must be so sick and tired of being sick and tired that we are prepared for serious action.

The 12-step program of Alcoholics Anonymous tells us, "Half measures avail us nothing." In other words, if we approach recovery with anything less than a full commitment, we're not likely to get very far.

In response to my work addiction, I go through periods where I compulsively set boundaries. For several years the pendulum swung wildly from one side to the other. I vowed to never again work evenings—a promise I've kept to this day. I set the number of appointments I would work per week and never exceeded it. I went to Friday meetings with my support group whether I was feeling well or I was on my deathbed. I clutched my recovery principles as though they were a lifeline in shark-infested waters.

Although I no longer have a desire to work evenings, I'm willing to do so on occasion when a true need arises. For years, I had to make a firm rule that I would not work evenings, regardless of the circumstances. I didn't trust my own impulses. If I hadn't set a hard-and-fast boundary, I might have given in to the excuses I had at the ready and slipped back into workaholism.

I wanted recovery badly. I wanted to get well. I was exhausted, anxious, and beginning to dislike my work. I didn't want to approach my recovery with half measures. I was willing to take out a knife and whittle away at my schedule, chopping off appointment after appointment until I began to feel healthy again.

How badly do you want to recover? Are you willing to go to any lengths to get healthy? Do you recognize that the half measures you tried in the past did nothing more than enable you to maintain your addiction?

Take a moment now and make a mental note of how desperately you want recovery. Jot down the half measures you've used in the past and the steps you'll take now to avoid cutting corners. Decide today that you'll go to any length necessary to recover from your addiction. Once you have taken that step, you will be on your way.

Doing the Work

Having the intention and desire, are you willing to do the work? Yes, I said *work*. It's a four-letter word. The healing process has no shortcuts. It requires practicing tried-and-true principles and understanding that your situation is not unique in that regard.

Although no gimmicks can speed you along the road to recovery, some established strategies have helped thousands recover from their addictions. I recommend that you embrace and employ them. These principles and practices constitute the work necessary for recovery.

Admitting addiction. It's time to stop hiding and admit your addiction. This is the starting point for every true recovery program. You've been lying to yourself for a long time, but the truth is what sets us free. It's time to acknowledge the truth about your addiction, including the effect it is having on your life and the lives of those around you.

Support group. Sharing your struggles with others is critical. In a support group, you will feel the freedom to admit your addiction and its long-lasting consequences. Others can help bear your burdens, and you can do the same for them. You no longer have to pretend that you've got it all together. You will have the opportunity to admit your fallibilities, and if you fail to do so, others will call you on your lies. These folks have "been there, done that" and can quickly see when you're acting too big for your britches. They'll keep you from slipping and help pick you up when you fall.

New friends and activities. Nearly everyone in recovery needs to jettison the negative friends they previously hung out with, admired, and emulated. They need to find people who are searching for a better way. You might find yours in a 12-step program, a Celebrate Recovery group, or some other structured organization where people agree to hold one another accountable for living a life of recovery. They will teach you how to have fun again in healthy and wholesome ways.

Withdrawal from your drug. We all have to go through some sort of withdrawal process. Obviously, this will be different for each of us. Withdrawal from methamphetamine addiction will be different from withdrawal from Oreo addiction. Withdrawal from sexual rituals will be different from withdrawal from compulsive participation in chat rooms. But regardless of the addiction, we all must go through a withdrawal process, and it may be very challenging.

Preparing for relapse. Although I hate to admit it, relapse is part of recovery. Some people not only experience relapse symptoms but slip fully back into addictive behavior. You must be prepared for this and know whom you will call when the urges sneak up on you and commandeer your brain.

Renewal of our minds. We all have "stinkin' thinkin'" and need to renew our minds. We all use rationalization, minimization, denial, and other thinking errors to keep our addictions cooking in high gear. We need the kind of transformation of the mind that comes from participation in support groups and programs, Scripture reading, and prayer. We need others who will confront us about our bad attitudes and slippery behavior, and we must submit to those who have our best interests in mind.

Practicing new recovery behavior. In your support group and while hanging out with healthy people, you discover positive ways of interacting with others. You learn what *normal* looks like. You learn healthy habits that guide your spending, sexuality, relaxation, expression of emotion, relating, eating, self-soothing, and of course, spiritual care. You begin the process of replacing old addictive behavior with new recovery behavior.

This is not an exhaustive list of recovery principles—only a starting point. Your particular recovery program will have its own set of principles and guidelines. But you absolutely must take your recovery seriously and recognize that you can't practice it in isolation.

Relapse or Recovery

A little compulsive behavior will serve you well during your recovery. A lackadaisical attitude is sure to trip you up, sending you reeling back into old addictive behaviors.

You are either in relapse or recovery. There is no middle ground. If you think you're in recovery but are not practicing the principles listed in this section of the book, you're kidding yourself. If you think you can practice half measures and still make progress, you're in denial.

Avoiding the Real Problem

Karin is 35, lively and animated, determined and persistent. She is a bright, educated, and innovative business woman. She is also an alcoholic who sought counseling services for herself and her husband because of their ongoing conflicts.

Walt is a contractor, familiar with the party scene. He enjoys a social life centered on beer and cocktails. Like Karin, he seems to have a high tolerance for alcohol and minimizes the destructive impact it has on their lives, in spite of the chronic problems in their relationship. Both are in denial.

Karin didn't volunteer any information about their drinking. Instead, she talked about "our horrendous fighting," sharing how they slipped easily into bickering and outright verbal brawls.

During their initial counseling session, I explored their drug and alcohol use. Both denied using drugs but did not hide the fact that they enjoy alcohol. Their consumption is an integral part of their social life and their fighting. After some questioning, they admitted that their quarrels are much worse when they've been drinking. This was not enough, however, to make either consider reducing or stopping their use of alcohol.

Karin comes by her alcoholism innocently enough. During her college years she drank with her sorority sisters. "Everyone was partying," she told me. She and Walt typically drink several cocktails before and after dinner each evening. She sees nothing wrong with this.

Interestingly, Karin had previously been in alcohol treatment after she was arrested for driving under the influence. She remains angry about her sentence and says, "I didn't need treatment. That's why I went back to drinking a month or two after the program ended." Walt, also in treatment several years ago, indicates he doesn't want to live without alcohol either.

After a few sessions, it became clear that Karin and Walt wanted to fight less, but had no interest in discussing the effects alcohol was having on their relationship. In fact, they denied the destructive impact of their drinking and were clearly in relapse.

A Picture of Recovery

Don's life is very different from Karin's and Walt's. A heavyset 40-year-old who works at the local paper mill, he too was arrested for DUI—in fact, he's had three of them. The first two, he says, did little to change his behavior.

Don sought professional help because he wants to renew visitation with his three young children, and counseling is the first step. He is open and willing to talk about his life.

"The third time was the charm," Don said. "I was stupid for a long time. I lost my wife, my house, my kids, and a good-paying job because of drinking. Now I have a new marriage and a new start, and I still have time to pull things together. Getting that last DUI was the best thing that ever happened to me."

"Why are things different this time?" I asked.

"I'm not sure," Don said. "Why does a person get it one time but not another? I don't think even you can answer that one, Doc."

I asked Don why he now wanted to have contact with his children after several years of ignoring them. He said that alcohol was no longer the center of his life. He wanted to rebuild his life and reestablish his relationship with his kids.

After the most recent DUI, he entered and completed an inpatient treatment program, but more importantly, Don practiced recovery principles. When I asked Don to tell me about his recovery, he described taking the following steps:

- He was attending at least three Alcoholics Anonymous meetings a week.
- He had a sponsor whom he called every few days to share positive and negative aspects of his week.
- He was attending church regularly and renewing his relationship with God.
- He was practicing the 12 steps and was currently doing assignments related to the third step in the process.
- He was attending couples' counseling with his wife to learn communication and conflict resolution skills.
- He had stopped seeing old friends with whom he used to drink.
- He was no longer going to places, such as taverns and the homes of former friends, which were "slippery places" for him.

Don had fully embraced recovery, and his new life reflected the changes he was making.

A False Start

Belinda's situation was different from Karin's, Walt's, and Don's. She initially came to counseling because of a history of depression. Previously a school counselor, she had retired several years ago, but she was having a tough time of it. Now in her early sixties, she wondered if she had made a mistake by retiring so young.

During counseling for her depression, she happened to bring up her spending habits, complaining that she never had enough money. She was single and survived on her school pension, but she always felt that she was living just beyond her means. This was a primary source of fear and frustration for her.

As we talked about her spending, Belinda readily agreed that it was out of control. She admitted that she shopped to combat her loneliness and also liked the rush she received from spending money. Sheepishly, she admitted going on shopping binges, only to return the majority of her purchases a few days later.

Belinda was unlike Karin and Walt in that she admitted having a problem. But like them, she refused to do anything about it.

"I'm not ready to change," she told me. "I know I have a problem. I suppose you could even call me a spending addict. I love my wardrobe, and shopping takes away some of my depression, even if it's just a temporary fix. I'm not going to give it up."

Belinda attended counseling for a few months and then stopped coming. I imagine that she continues to shop to mask her depression. Perhaps her depression isn't bad enough for her to change the factors in her life causing it. Perhaps facing her addiction is too frightening, and she's not willing to be completely honest with herself about it. Her depression feeds her addiction, and her addiction feeds her depression.

Belinda is active in her addiction. Though never formally in recovery, she is, in a sense, in relapse. She is taking responsibility for her addiction and thus is in relapse. Her only hope for significant change is to face her problems and map out a plan of recovery.

Slippery Places

Every addict has slippery slopes—people, places, and feelings that tempt us to fall back into addictive behaviors. If you aren't keenly aware of your slippery places, and if you don't possess an almost sacred respect for their power, you're in trouble.

For Belinda, her slippery place involved being alone on the weekends, which left her lonely and depressed. She disliked being single but did little to seek healthy companionship and dating. Feeling lonely and sorry for herself, she would head for the mall.

Karin and Walt enjoyed hanging out with friends, with alcohol playing a central role. They weren't ready to admit that social gatherings, with alcohol present, were slippery places that led not only to drinking but also to fighting.

Don is the only one of the group in recovery. He understands the importance of not hanging around the old places with the old friends, doing the old things that set him up to drink. He is actively making new sober friends. He seeks out others who are working a recovery program. They watch out for one another and acknowledge that they will be sorely tempted to relapse.

As you consider working a recovery program, you need to recognize the situations that are likely to lead to relapse. The Scriptures tell us, "If you think you are standing firm, be careful that you don't fall" (1 Corinthians 10:12). We're all capable of being caught off guard and need to fully understand the places and people that pose a danger.

Relapse Prevention

Understanding your slippery places is one of the key components of developing a clear and concise relapse prevention plan. Without it, recovery is not possible.

Once we acknowledge that relapse is a part of recovery, we can guard against setbacks by establishing several strategies:

- Write out a thorough description of the steps that led you into addictive behavior. Knowing how you got to where you are will help you understand what you must eliminate in order to live an addiction-free life. What were the attitudes and beliefs that reinforced your addictive behavior?

- Write down the names of people and places you will avoid in your effort to eliminate addictive behavior from your life. Specifically, list the slippery places that are most likely to lead to relapse.

- List the new people and places that you will incorporate into your life and that will help steer you toward healthy recovery. Write down people's names and phone numbers and vow to reach out for support when you need it. Don't wait until a crisis erupts before contacting your support network.

- Write out the names of the recovery or support groups that you will attend on a regular basis. Where do they meet and on which days? How will you begin to establish new rituals in your life through your participation in these groups?

- List what you will do with all the time you previously dedicated to addictive behavior. You need structure in your life, especially at the start, so establish a weekly schedule that keeps you busy and focused. You can loosen up after you've been in recovery a while.

- Note the areas of your life that need to be strengthened. Do you need to make new friends? Do you need an enriched spiritual life?

Your relapse prevention plan can be a valuable tool for mapping out your ideal life. Be creative.

Climbing out of the Holes

Imagine you're walking down the street. Out of nowhere a gigantic hole of relapse plops down in front of you, and you stumble in. Now what?

You climb out.

This may sound overly simplistic, but it's the best advice I can give. You'd be amazed at how many people wallow in self-pity when they relapse. Some decide that since they've fallen off the wagon, they might as well enjoy it. Others believe the hole is so deep that there can be no way out.

When you fall into one of those holes, climb out and get on your way as quickly as possible. Even those of us with solid, well thought-out relapse prevention plans can fall into a hole now and then. Expect it to happen. Relapse is not a moral failure, nor is it a sin for which you need to flagellate yourself. Get on with the recovery process.

Progress, Not Perfection

Why do I ask that you take your relapse in stride? Not because I want you to take it lightly, but because experts tell us that a high percentage of recovering addicts *will* relapse. There is no such thing as a fail-safe, mistake-proof recovery program. We need to remind ourselves again and again that we are aiming for progress, not perfection.

If we mistakenly rely on what we believe to be a surefire recovery program, our only companions will be loneliness and failure. No program is perfect.

Comparing ourselves with others can also be very harmful. When we think about Joe, who's been in Celebrate Recovery for ten years, leads classes, and supposedly never has a bad day, we are tempted to try to emulate him. But if we do that, we'll be in trouble. First, Joe has bad days. Trust me on this. Second, he's been in the program ten years, and you may have been in it three months. Trying to emulate his every move is neither realistic nor productive.

Having said that, I do want you to learn from those who have walked the path you are now on. Those who have worked a recovery program for years and seem to be incorporating the principles into their lives can serve as sponsors and inspirational guides. Don't, however, try to follow their footsteps exactly. It won't work. Your life and your circumstances are unique.

Because we strive for progress, not perfection, you should measure your gains in three-month increments, not day by day. As the months go by, are you faithful in attending your support group? Are you reading helpful materials, including Scripture, and allowing your mind to be transformed? Are you making calls to healthy friends when in the dumps? Are you avoiding slippery places? Do you forgive yourself when you relapse? Do you catch your relapses early?

This is a recovery program. These are the things we can do to get healthier. Expecting minute-to-minute progress is not helpful.

Always Recovering, Never Recovered

Even after years of recovery, a tickle of the old behavior pattern may remain. You might have a dream or fond memory of the "good old days," which of course weren't so good. But the craving brain may send us signals now and again, just to see if the temptation takes hold.

Some experts disagree with me on this point. Some believe we can be fully cured. Some people seem to have been cured.

I'm not one of them. I always feel the tug back into the deeper waters of work and approval addiction. I've accepted, more or less, that I'll always have to deal with these challenges.

So how about this? If you, through spiritual or other means, obtain a complete and total recovery and never experience the old urges again, and if your mind is miraculously cured of those patterns of stinkin' thinkin', I ask that you do one thing for me—*celebrate!*

The vast majority of us need to come to grips with the fact that we'll always struggle with our cravings. We'll be like the apostle Paul, who lamented that he was forever doing what he wished he didn't do and not doing what he wished he did do.

In all likelihood, you're like the rest of us: You will be challenged every day to do your best. Most likely, there will be no magic tricks, just the growing ability to choose to avoid engaging in addictive behavior. This boils down to practicing your recovery principles on a daily basis. Today, make the choice not to engage in addictive behavior. Tomorrow, refuse again.

I don't want this to sound discouraging, but life is messy. You need to acknowledge that and prepare for it.

Irwin Kula and Linda Loewenthal, in their book *Yearnings,* acknowledge that we, along with our biblical ancestors, are always transgressing and recovering, and we must accept this.

> The Bible isn't prescribing sin but rather describing the human journey. The Bible understands that as hurtful as transgressions can be, there can be no life journey without them. Most of us lead conventional lives. We want to avoid the discomforts that arise from complications. But, the full, creative life must be open to unpredictability.[1]

The path to recovery is a path of unpredictability.

Grace

All you can do is all you can do. Where we end, God begins.

Our recovery and our relapses will include times when we will be disappointed, angry, and frustrated.

Sitting with my men's group, year after year, and saying the Serenity Prayer at the end of each meeting was a sublime experience. It didn't save me. It didn't stop the cravings. But it did offer me moments of peace in the midst of the storms that racked my life. I felt God's grace intensely.

Each of us is engaged in struggles. Some wrestle with drug addiction or alcoholism. Some battle with food, eating too much or too little. Others are challenged by gambling, Internet gaming, or sexual cravings. Some are at the mercy of materialism or excessive work. Many of us give up our own identities in order to seek someone else's approval. These are all authentic struggles.

Right smack dab in the middle of these struggles we can experience God's grace and feel it carrying us along. This grace will elevate us on our journey. Gerald May, in his book *Addiction and Grace,* explains:

But indeed God is in it with us all along, and wherever our choices are enabled to remain simple and our intent remains solid, empowerment comes through grace. There is little else we can do except keep on trying, and looking for God's invitations and seeking simplicity.[2]

I am still in recovery, though my path today is far easier than it was years ago. My seven years in the support group were invaluable to me. Those men helped me see that I'm in the same boat as most others—we're all addicts, and many of us are in search of healing. I still need God's grace to avoid slipping back into workaholism. My strength is not enough, but God's strength and grace are sufficient.

I'll close this book the way we closed our men's group, offering you the Serenity Prayer. My deepest wish is that it will grace you on your journey of recovery.

> *God, grant me the serenity to accept the things I*
> *cannot change, the courage to change the things I*
> *can, and the wisdom to know the difference.*
> *Living one day at a time; enjoying one moment*
> *at a time;*
> *Accepting hardships as the pathway to peace;*
> *Taking, as He did, this sinful world as it is, not*
> *as I would have it;*
> *Trusting that He will make all things right if*
> *I surrender to His will;*
> *That I may be reasonably happy in this life and*
> *supremely happy with Him forever in the next.*
> *Amen.*

—Attributed to Rheinhold Niehbuhr

Notes

Chapter 1—A Parade of Everyday Addicts

1. M. Scott Peck, *The Road Less Traveled* (New York: Simon & Schuster, 1978), 16.
2. Gerald May, *Addiction and Grace* (San Francisco: HarperSanFrancisco, 1988), 83.
3. May, *Addiction and Grace,* 84.

Chapter 2—Distant Elephants

1. Cited in Gregory L. Jantz, *Turning the Tables on Gambling* (Colorado Springs: Waterbrook Press, 2001), p.64.
2. Nora Ephron, *I Feel Bad About My Neck* (New York: Knopf, 2006), 3.
3. Jeff and Debra Jay, *Love First* (Center City, MN: Hazelden Foundation, 2000), 25.
4. Harriet Lerner, *The Dance of Deception* (New York: HarperCollins, 1993), 14.
5. M. Scott Peck, *The Road Less Traveled* (New York: Simon & Schuster, 1978), 44.
6. Dan Allender, *The Healing Path* (Colorado Springs: Waterbrook Press, 1999), 237.
7. Allender, *The Healing Path,* 243.

Chapter 3—DENIAL—Don't Even Notice I Am Lying

1. Lance Dodes, *The Heart of Addiction* (New York: HarperCollins, 2002), 102.
2. Gerald May, *Addiction and Grace* (San Francisco: HarperSanFrancisco, 1988), 43.
3. Stanton Peele, *7 Tools to Beat Addiction* (New York: Three Rivers Press, 2004), 91.

Chapter 4—The Anatomy of Addictions

1. Anne Wilson Schaef, *When Society Becomes an Addict* (New York: Harper & Row, 1987), 23.
2. Norman Doidge, *The Brain That Changes Itself* (New York: Viking, 2007), 106.
3. Archibald Hart, *Thrilled to Death* (Nashville: Nelson, 2007), 97.
4. Hart, *Thrilled to Death,* 102.
5. Julia Cameron, *The Artist's Way* (New York: Tarcher, 1992), 164.
6. Patrick Carnes, *Out of the Shadows* (Minneapolis: CompCare, 1983), 9.

Chapter 5—Under the Influence

1. James Milam and Katherine Ketcham, *Under the Influence* (New York: Bantam, 1983), 40.
2. Jennifer Hurley, ed., *Drug Abuse: Opposing Viewpoints* (San Diego: Greenhaven Press, 2000), 36.
3. Donald Goodwin, *Alcoholism: The Facts* (New York: Oxford University Press, 1976).

4. Statistics from the 2004 National Survey on Drug Use and Health, series H-27, no. SMA 05-4061. (Rockville, MD: Office of Applied Studies).

Chapter 6—Measuring Up

1. Kay Sheppard, *Food Addiction* (Deerfield Beach, FL: Health Communications, 1993), 3.

2. Sheppard, *Food Addiction*, 4-5.

3. Jim Kirkpatrick and Paul Caldwell, *Eating Disorders* (New York: Firefly Books, 2001), 94.

4. Kirkpatrick and Caldwell, *Eating Disorders*, 96.

Chapter 7—Sexual Sanity

1. Patrick Carnes, *Don't Call It Love* (New York: Bantam Books, 1991), 30.

2. Stephen Arterburn, *Addicted to Love* (New York: Vine Books, 1995).

3. Anne Wilson Schaef, *Escape from Intimacy* (San Francisco: Harper & Row, 1989), 12.

4. Carnes, *Don't Call It Love*, 307-8.

Chapter 8—Not Until Your Work Is Done!

1. Ruth Haley Barton, *Invitation to Solitude and Silence* (Downers Grove, IL: Inter-Varsity Press, 2004), 25-26.

2. www.allianceforchildhood.org/projects/play/index.htm.

Chapter 9—Chasing Your Losses

1. Ronald Ruden, *The Craving Brain* (New York: HarperCollins, 1997), 196.

2. Bernard Horn, *Gambling: Opposing Viewpoints* (San Diego: Greenhaven Press, 2000), 62.

3. Anne Wilson Schaef, *When Society Becomes an Addict* (New York: Harper & Row, 1987), 22.

4. Lance Dodes, *The Heart of Addiction* (New York: HarperCollins, 2002), 201.

Chapter 10—When Pleasing Others Is Hurting You

1. Melodie Beattie, *Codependent No More* (Center City, MN: Hazeldon, 1987), 36.

2. Pia Mellody, *Facing Love Addiction* (San Francisco: HarperSanFrancisco, 1992), 3.

3. Mellody, *Facing Love Addiction*, 4-5.

4. Barry Weinhold, Janae Weinhold, and John Bradshaw, *Breaking Free of the Co-dependency Trap* (Walpole, NH: Stillpoint, 1989), 9.

5. Joyce Meyer, *Approval Addiction* (New York: Time Warner Book Group, 2005), vii.

6. Meyer, *Approval Addiction*, 161.

7. Maya Angelou, *The Heart of a Woman* (New York: Bantam, 1981), 2.

8. Meyer, *Approval Addiction*, 96.

Chapter 11—Facing Our Addictions

1. Gerald May, *Addiction and Grace* (San Francisco: HarperSanFrancisco, 1988), 95.

2. May, *Addiction and Grace*, 96.

Chapter 12—Letting Go

1. William Bridges, *The Way of Transitions* (Cambridge: Perseus, 2001), 58.

2. Brennan Manning, *Reflections for Ragamuffins* (San Francisco: HarperSanFrancisco, 1998), 231.

3. M. Scott Peck, *The Road Less Traveled* (New York: Simon & Schuster, 1978), 44.

4. Melodie Beattie, *The Language of Letting Go* (New York: Harper & Row, 1990), 66.

5. Susan Jeffers, *Feel the Fear and Do It Anyway* (New York: Fawcett Columbine, 1987), 25.

6. Bridges, *The Way of Transitions*, 204.

Chapter 13—Healing Our Addictions

1. Irwin Kula and Linda Loewenthal, *Yearnings* (New York: Hyperion, 2006), 118.

2. Gerald May, *Addiction and Grace* (San Francisco: HarperSanFrancisco, 1988), 178.

Marriage Intensives

Dr. David Hawkins has developed a unique and powerful ministry to couples who need more than weekly counseling. In a waterfront cottage on beautiful Puget Sound in the Pacific Northwest, Dr. Hawkins works with one couple at a time in Marriage Intensives over three days, breaking unhealthy patterns of conflict while acquiring new, powerful skills that can empower husbands and wives to restore their marriage to the love they once knew.

If you feel stuck in a relationship fraught with conflict and want to make positive changes working with Dr. Hawkins individually or as a couple, please contact him at 360.490.5446 or learn more about his Marriage Intensives at www.YourRelationshipDoctor.com.

Call Dr. Hawkins for a professional phone consultation, or schedule him and his wife, Christie, for your next speaking engagement or marriage retreat.

Other Great Harvest House Books
by Dr. David Hawkins

(To read sample chapters, visit www.harvesthousepublishers.com.)

When Pleasing Others Is Hurting You

When you begin to forfeit your own God-given calling and identity in an unhealthy desire to please others, you move from servanthood to codependency. This helpful guide can get you back on track.

Dealing with the CrazyMakers in Your Life

People who live in chaos and shrug off responsibility can drive you crazy. If you are caught up in a disordered person's life, Dr. Hawkins helps you set boundaries, confront the behavior, and find peace.

Nine Critical Mistakes Most Couples Make

Dr. Hawkins shows that complex relational problems usually spring from nine destructive habits couples fall into, and he offers practical suggestions for changing the way husbands and wives relate to each other.

When Trying to Change Him Is Hurting You

Dr. Hawkins offers practical suggestions for women who want to improve the quality of their relationships by helping the men in their lives become healthier and more fun to live with.

When the Man in Your Life Can't Commit

With empathy and insight Dr. Hawkins uncovers the telltale signs of commitment failure, why the problem exists, and how you can respond to create a life with the commitment-phobic man you love.

Are You Really Ready for Love

As a single, you are faced with a challenge: When love comes your way, will you be ready? Dr. Hawkins encourages you to spend less energy looking for the perfect mate and more energy becoming a person who can enter wholeheartedly into intimate relationships.

The Relationship Doctor's Prescription for Living Beyond Guilt
Dr. Hawkins explains the difference between real guilt, false guilt, shame, and conviction, bringing these feelings into the light and demonstrating how they can reveal the true causes of emotional pain.

The Relationship Doctor's Prescription for Better Communication in Your Marriage
Communication is an art. Couples thrive when they listen deeply, understand completely, and validate one another compassionately. But many couples try to win arguments, not to understand each other. This user-friendly manual reveals common but ineffective patterns of relating and teaches new skills in the art of communication.

The Relationship Doctor's Prescription for Building Your Child's Self-Image
Dr. Hawkins describes what positive self-image is, what it is not, and how to help kids develop a Christlike confidence without conceit. You'll find practical descriptions of children's psychological needs, harmful parenting habits to avoid, and constructive ways to help your children build a healthy self-image.

How to Get Your Husband's Attention
She says one thing, but he hears something entirely different. What can you do to bridge the communication gap? This inspiring guide provides straightforward answers and practical solutions to encourage and motivate you to press through to the ultimate goal: greater intimacy in marriage.

Rerelease of *Saying It So He'll Listen*

The Power of Emotional Decision Making
"Energy in motion"—that's how Dr. Hawkins describes emotions. He shows how emotions can help you discern what is most important, determine what is missing in your life, and discover how God is leading you in new directions.